dancing on the ARK

FACING CHANGE IN UNCERTAIN TIMES
WHAT EVERY NOAH OUGHT TO KNOW

To Daign [signature] Kelly Walker

KELLY WALKER

KW Productions©

Canadian Cataloguing in Publication Data
Walker, Kelly, 1941–
Dancing on the Ark: Facing Change In
Uncertain Times (What every Noah ought to know)

Includes bibliographical references.
ISBN 0-9680315-3-6

1. Life change events—Psychological aspects.   I. Title

BF637.L53W34 2000   155.9'3   C00-900419-X

Published in Canada by
KW Productions
511 Pinegrove Avenue, P.O. Box 64013
Oakville, Ontario, Canada L6K 2C0
1-800-438-3422

Printing
Webcom Limited, Toronto

Cover Illustration
Laurie Quinn

Cover Concept, Book Design, Editing and Typesetting
Judy Anderson

Author Photo
Denise Grant Photography

To Ray,

Marjorie,

Sally and Alexandra

for all their Sacred Acts

Kelly Walker is an author, speaker, singer-songwriter and recording artist. He spent twenty years as a Dominican Friar and then forged a new life in the public arena after leaving the priesthood. His best-selling first book, Loss of Soul: Burnout, is in its second printing.

The author now lives in the beautiful Hockley Hills north of Toronto.

CONTENTS

And when old words die out on the tongue,
new melodies break forth from the heart;
and where the old tracks are lost,
new country is revealed with its wonders.

—Rabindranath Tagore, Gitanjali

INTRODUCTION

Change feels difficult. Each time I am faced with the prospect of change that is forced upon me, I go into resistance mode. However, my generation has faced more change in the past fifty years than has all of society in five hundred. What feels hard has become normal for us. Most of us are even good at it. But it still feels hard.

By the time we reach fifty, some of us have lived in twenty different dwellings, been through several major relationships, had many jobs, (and possibly even now are searching for new careers). We may have had cancer or HIV scares, lived through wars and suffered various crashes. And we have survived. Yet, every new challenge is a challenge! It is difficult to overcome the terrors and the fears that unsolicited change brings.

We seem to live between trapezes and in such transitions we need direction, strategies, and above all, courage. I feel I have lived all my life between trapezes. And I know it's not over yet.

I am writing these pages to help you hang in with peace. I am likely writing them for myself as well, and for the same reasons. Through stories, theory and encouragement, I hope you will gain some of the energy you need to pass through the turbulent waters of transformation, out of which all good living grows.

There is no one theory that is adequate to proclaim "the way." You must design your own survival package to deal with change. It is through the stories of the elders, the mythologies that support survival and the power of your own inner energy that you will be able to pass through the valleys that lead to new tomorrows.

Most of the stories in this book come from my own experiences as a therapist, musician, artist, friend and happy human forever in transition. Generally, the names and circumstances have been altered. References to Hebrew and Christian literature are good and cherished tales that have helped me on my journey. I hope they will work for you as well. I hope you also discover some of your own.

Be still. Read on. Rest. And talk to loads of people about it all. They are doing it too! Every day!

YOU ARE NOT ALONE IN THIS!

Kelly Walker,
Ash Croft in the Hockley Hills, Ontario
October, 1999

The Times

Change is the law of life. And those who look only at the past or present are certain to miss the future.

—*John Fitzgerald Kennedy*

Back on the eve of the twentieth century, the French historian, Alexis de Tocqueville, wrote that in a democracy every generation is a new civilization. With the speed of generational turnover now at the end of the twentieth century, chances are that in any one household in North America there are several civilizations living side by side. Witness the music, the worldviews, the hair, the clothing. Anyone with a child in Grade Nine and another in Grade Twelve knows only too well that they are living with two civilizations. Their dress, their language and their worldviews speak of different ways of being. We no longer witness civilization differences only in countries other than our own. We live with them daily, intermingling one with another.

These are strange threshold times. Ancient mythologies speak of demons dwelling around the threshold of a house (that was why the bride was carried over the threshold). We know only too well that the demonic is alive and well on the threshold of change. Fear, insecurity, self doubt, phantoms from some far off past often become ominous creatures from the dark. What powers were appeased in ancient times by garlic, a phallus, or a statue to some god or goddess, now require many more powerful protectors.

Coming out of what seemed a time of stability, many of us feel put upon to have to deal with change at all, much less to grapple with the demons that make it hard to move beyond our comfort zones.

The truth is that there has never been a time of stability in the history of the universe. If there had been even one single moment of stability in the history of time, we would have ceased to be. Yet we forget that every living thing is constantly in flux. The ancient peoples and the philosophers of old knew that. We have forgotten the wisdom of the ancients as we nationalized, nuclearized and privatized in the twentieth century. In a time when expansiveness was most possible, in many ways—perhaps out of fear—we became provincial and static. The unknown and the uncertain sometimes petrify us.

On the one hand we are petrified. On the other hand, we are masters of change. We, of all the generations born on this earth, have had to *just do it*! Before one product got to the shelf, we were already introduced to the next. Change freaks us but at the same time piques us.

In the past ten years, every government, every company, every organization has radically modified its way of being as well as its self-understanding. It has been necessary. New needs, new economic realities, new personnel requirements and new worldviews have predicated the changes required. We have been moulded, folded and scolded into something we never imagined before.

•   •   •

RECENTLY, I WAS DELIVERING A TALK to a gathering of one hundred or so men and women from one of the branches of the Canadian government. They were sitting at round tables— together.

That's new. None of us was trained to engage in such dangerous activity. Women sat together in bees. Men gathered together in ranks. We all sat in rows in school, in church and in the theatre. Together? At round tables? That is radical, revolutionary and for some, at times, crazy-making behaviour! It requires collaboration, listening, sharing feelings and democratization. Males were never prepared for any of that. It is traumatizing and uncomfortable for many. But we are doing it.

•   •   •

MOST OF US NOW USE COMPUTERS. Some of us live in an

old paradigm and use a computer as though it were a type-writer. That is the beginning and end of it for some of us. New technology—old paradigm.

Our children live in the new paradigm and are very fluent with the new technology. Very few in my generation know how a computer works. Can you remember how terrified you were when you first touched one? When they told you at the office that you would have to learn how to do it? But you did! You even mastered some system that was a new language to you. By the time you had mastered it at all, the newest version had appeared and you were encouraged to master the newest skills. For the most part, you have been quite good at moving along as needed.

• • •

I HAVE INHERITED THREE of the most marvellous grand-children, Madelena, Kristin and Joseph Patrick. A few weeks ago, they came to visit with my boy, Rob, and my daugh-ter-in-law, JoAnn. The eldest children came to me and said, "Papa, can we play with your computer?"

I stiffened and told them that computers were not made to be played with. I told them that it was my principal work in-strument and that it was not for children. For me, my com-puter is a typewriter. I process words on it.

For the children, however, it is not that at all. Not one of them even knows what a typewriter is. They have never even seen one. They have never processed words. For them it is a tool used to access another world (of which I am unaware). As I stated earlier, we are two civilizations!

• • •

WE HAD A YARD SALE on our beautiful street in Parkdale a few years ago. We had placed some records on the table to sell for fifty cents. A young girl approached me and asked me what they were. I said "records."

She asked me what records were used for. I said, "Why, to

play."

"Play what?" she said.

"Music," I said.

"How?" she asked.

"On a record player," I replied.

"What is that?"

She had never seen one.

•   •   •

WHAT IS A NUN? I remember walking through the streets of Montreal in the sixties and meeting a hundred or so nuns walking two by two, hands folded, eyes down, out for "recreation." Now there is nary a sign that nuns exist in Montreal. My grandchildren truly have never seen one. I saw them every day at their age!

•   •   •

A SHORT TIME AGO, once again I was in Montreal—a city of churches. Before me stood an impressive old building, which housed a parish community that used to have about 1500 people at each Mass. There were two recent signs on the building; BINGO and FOR SALE. What was the Sunday duty of millions of *Quebecois* until 1967 had now become the practice of very few. The Anglican bishop of Montreal admitted to me awhile back that he had it better than the Catholic bishop because his churches were small enough to be transformed into condos or libraries. Strange, threshold times.

•   •   •

MOST OF US HAVE EXPERIENCED outhouses at one time or another in our lives. One woman in Saskatchewan told me that when the indoor plumbing was introduced on their farm, her dad insisted that the indoor plumbing—the pipes—extend out to the outhouse. According to him, that was never meant to be inside. Paradigm shift!

We have gone from outhouse to water closet to two to four

toilets in less than fifty years. That was probably an easy shift for most of us.

• • •

I WAS WALKING UP YONGE STREET in Toronto with an elderly friend a few years ago. She was wearing a green leather pantsuit, hair dyed red, and was bedecked with ruby red lipstick. As we approached Bloor Street, in the fashionable Yorkville district, she leaned over to me and confessed that her mother would have had great difficulty seeing her so—she was not wearing a hat or gloves (required clothing until the sixties on Bloor Street). The leather, hair and lipstick were incidental!

• • •

IN THE DANCE OF LIFE that gets us from Point A to Point B, it is better to have anchors along the way. In my life, there have been people I could hook onto. They gave me inspiration and courage by their example, sometimes by words and often from stories they graciously shared with me about their life passages.

Most civilizations have had their paths cleared a bit by the myths and stories that were told by the elders and sages. Our civilization has experienced a poverty in this regard. We threw the elders out with the bath water and have eliminated most religious myths from our landscape as we dumped organized religion. But now we need supports in this strange new land that we venture into. It would be helpful to us, I believe, both for our peace and for our survival that we recover some of that ancient wisdom for our time.

One story that has always fascinated me has been that of Noah and the Ark. I propose it to you as one of the old tales that our ancestors have left us from their survival packages. First, listen to the story and then try, as I will, to get the meat out of it. It may give you some clues as to how to proceed on your own journey.

Your Passages: An Inventory

1. Write down some of the changes you can think of that indicate you have lived within several paradigms to date. Write them down so that you can see them before you.

2. Here are a few questions for you to write down as well.

How old are you now? _____

How old will you be in 5 years? _____

In 10 years? _____

In 15 years? _____

3. List major changes in your lifetime:

Conception–1 year _____

_____

_____

2–5 years _____

_____

_____

6–12 years _____

_____

_____

13–18 years _____

_____

_____

19–24 years _____

_____

_____

25–34 years _____

_____

_____

35–49 years _____

_____

_____

50–64 years _____

_____

_____

65 years and beyond _____

_____

_____

The Story of Noah and the Ark

Change and growth take place when a person has risked himself and dares to become involved with experimenting with his own life.

—*Herbert Otto*

T his ancient story is taken from the Hebrew literature. It served as a guide to a nomadic tribe that had to face change daily as it sought safe haven and good land in the midst of what was often desert. This story was and still is a sign-post for a people who have had to learn to live in a holding pattern in the foreign land, until the dream of gathering "next year in Jerusalem" could become a reality. The story of Noah and his family is so important to them. It may become so for you, as well. Here it is.

THE LORD SAW that the wickedness of humankind was great in the earth, and that every inclination of the thoughts of their hearts was only evil continually. And the Lord was sorry that he had made humankind on the earth and it grieved him to his heart. So the Lord said, "I will blot out from the earth the human beings I have created—people together with animals and creeping things and birds of the air, for I am sorry that I have made them." But Noah found favour in the sight of the Lord.

These are the descendants of Noah. Noah was a righteous man, blameless in his generation; Noah walked with God. And Noah had three sons, Shem, Ham and Japheth.

Now the earth was corrupt in God's sight, and the earth was filled with violence. And God saw that the earth was corrupt; for all flesh had corrupted its ways upon the earth.

And God said to Noah, "I have determined to make an end of all flesh, for the earth is filled with violence because of them; now I am going to destroy them along with the earth.

Make yourself an Ark of cypress wood; make rooms in the Ark, and cover it inside and out with pitch. This is how you are to make it: the length of the Ark three hundred cubits, its width fifty cubits, and its height thirty cubits. Make a roof for the Ark and finish it to a cubit above; and put the door of the Ark on its side; make it with lower and second and third decks.

For my part, I am going to bring a flood of waters on the earth, to destroy from under heaven all flesh in which is the breath of life; everything that is on the earth shall die.

But I will establish my covenant with you; and you shall come into the Ark, you, your sons, your wife and your sons' wives with you. And of every living thing, of all flesh, you shall bring two of every kind into the Ark, to keep them according to their kinds, and of the animals according to their kinds, of every creeping thing of the ground according to its kind, two of every kind shall come in to you, to keep them alive. Also take with you every kind of food that is eaten, and store it up; and it shall serve as food for you and for them.

Noah did this; he did all that God commanded him.

Then the Lord said to Noah, "Go into the Ark, you and your household, for I have seen that you alone are righteous before me in this generation. Take with you seven pairs of all clean animals, the male and its mate; and a pair of animals that are not clean, the male and its mate; and seven pairs of the birds of the air also, male and female, to keep their kind alive on the face of the earth. For in seven days I will send rain on the earth for forty days and forty nights; and every living thing that I have made I will blot out from the face of the ground. And Noah did all that the Lord had commanded him.

Noah was six hundred years old when the flood of waters came on the earth. And Noah with his sons and his wife and his sons' wives went into the Ark to escape the waters of the flood. Of clean animals, and of animals that are not clean, and of birds , and of everything that creeps on the ground, two and two, male and female, went into the Ark with Noah, as God had commanded Noah.

And after seven days the waters of the flood came on the earth. In the six hundredth year of Noah's life, in the second month, on the seventeenth day of the month, on that day all the fountains of the great deep burst forth, and the windows of the heavens were opened. The rain fell on the earth forty days and forty nights. On the very same day Noah with his sons, Shem and Ham and Japheth, and Noah's wife and the three wives of his sons entered the Ark, they and every wild animal of every kind, and all domestic animals of every kind, and every creeping thing that creeps on the earth, and every bird of every kind—every bird, every winged creature. They went into the Ark with Noah, two and two of all flesh in which there was breath of life. And those that entered, male and female of all flesh, went in as God had commanded him; and the Lord shut him in.

The flood continued forty days on the earth; and the waters increased and bore up the Ark, and it rose high above the earth. The waters swelled and increased greatly on the earth; and the Ark floated on the face of the waters. The waters swelled so mightily on the earth that all the high mountains under the whole heaven were covered; the waters welled above the mountains, covering them fifteen cubits deep. And all flesh died that moved on the earth, birds, domestic animals, wild animals, all swarming creatures that swarm on the earth and all human beings; everything on dry land in whose nostrils was the breath of life died. He blotted out every living thing that was on the face of the ground, human beings and animals and creeping things and birds of the air; they were blotted out from the earth. Only Noah was left, and those that were with him on the Ark. And the waters swelled on the earth for one hundred fifty days.

But God remembered Noah and all the wild animals

and all the domestic animals that were with him on the Ark. And God made a wind blow over the earth, and the waters subsided; the fountains of the deep and the windows of the heavens were closed, the rain from the heavens was restrained and the waters gradually receded from the earth. At the end of one hundred fifty days the waters had abated; and in the seventh month, on the seventeenth day of the month, the Ark came to rest on the mountains of Ararat. The waters continued to abate until the tenth month; in the tenth month, on the first day of the month, the tops of the mountains appeared. At the end of forty days Noah opened the window of the Ark that he had made and sent out the raven; and it went to and fro until the waters were dried up from the earth, Then he sent out the dove from him, to see if the waters had subsided from the face of the ground; but the dove found no place to set its foot, and it returned to him to the Ark, for the waters were still on the face of the whole earth. So he put his hand and took it and brought it into the Ark with him. He waited another seven days, and again he sent out the dove from the Ark; and the dove came back to him in the evening, and there in its beak was a freshly plucked olive leaf; so Noah knew that the waters had subsided from the earth. Then he waited another seven days, and sent out the dove; and it did not return to him any more.

In the six hundred first year, in the first month, the first day of the month, the waters were dried up from the earth; and Noah removed the covering of the Ark, and looked, and saw that the face of the ground was drying. In the second month, on the twenty-seventh day of the month, the earth was dry.

Then God said to Noah, "Go out of the Ark and bring your wife and your sons and your sons' wives with you. Bring out with you every living thing that is with you of all flesh-eating birds and animals and every creeping thing that creeps on the earth." So Noah went out with his sons and his wife and his sons' wives. And every animal, every creeping thing, and every bird, everything that moves on the earth, went out of the Ark by families.

Then Noah built an altar to the Lord and took of every clean animal and of every clean bird and offered burnt offerings on the altar. And when the Lord smelled the pleasing odour, the Lord said in his heart, "I will never again curse the ground because of humankind, for the inclination of the human heart is evil from youth; nor will I ever again destroy every living creature as I have done. As long as the earth endures, seedtime and harvest, cold and heat, summer and winter, day and night, shall not cease." God blessed Noah and his sons, and said to them, "Be fruitful and multiply, and fill the earth. The fear and dread of you shall rest on every animal of the earth, and on every bird of the air, on everything that creeps on the ground, and on all fish of the sea; into your hand they are delivered. Every moving thing that lives shall be food for you; and just as I gave you the green plants, I give you everything. Only, you shall not eat flesh with its life, that is, with its blood. For your own lifeblood I will surely require a reckoning; from every animal I will require it and from human beings, each one for the blood of another, I will require a reckoning for human life. Whoever sheds the blood of a human, by a human shall that person's blood be shed; for in his own image God made humankind. And you, be fruitful and multiply, abound on the earth and multiply in it."

Then God said to Noah and to his sons with him, "As for me, I am establishing my covenant with every living creature that is with you, the birds, the domestic animals and every animal of the earth with you, as many as came out of the Ark. I establish my covenant with you, that never again shall all flesh be cut off by the waters of a flood, and never again shall there be a flood to destroy the earth."

And God said, "This is the sign of the covenant that I make between me and you and every living creature that is with you, for all future generations: I have set my bow in the clouds, and it shall be a sign of the covenant between me and the earth.

"When I bring clouds over the earth and the bow is seen in the clouds, and I will remember my covenant that is between me and you and every living creature of all flesh; and the waters shall never again become a flood to destroy all flesh. When the bow is in the clouds, I will see it and remember the everlasting covenant between God and every living creature of all flesh that is on the earth."

The sons of Noah who went out of the Ark were Shem, Ham, and Japheth. Ham was the father of Canaan. These three were the sons of Noah; and from these the whole earth was peopled. Noah a man of the soil, was the first to plant a vineyard. He drank some of the wine and became drunk, and he lay uncovered in his tent. And Ham, the father of Canaan, saw the nakedness of his father, and told his two brothers outside. Then Shem and Japheth took a garment, laid it on both their shoulders, and walked backward and covered the nakedness of their father; their faces were turned away, and they did not see their father's nakedness. When Noah awoke from his wine and knew that his youngest son had done to him, he said, "Cursed be Canaan; lowest of slaves shall he be to his brothers."

He also said, "Blessed by the Lord my God be Shem; and let Canaan be his slave. May God make space for Japheth, and let him live in the tents of Shem; and let Canaan be his slave." After the flood Noah lived three hundred fifty years. All the days of Noah were nine hundred fifty years; and he died.

• • •

THAT IS THE STORY of Noah and the Ark, which has captured the imagination of countless generations of humans as they have passed through their various deluges. Each of us becomes the story as our life unfolds.

Heroes

I won't change. I will be buried in this habit. I know God called me to be in this Order and the habit is as much a part of that as is the rule. I'll not change.
—Dominican Nun, 1971

I know that we must be poor with the poorest and stand firm with the wealthy who can help with the changes. We must adapt. This new day has never been before. The habit does not make the monk!
—Same Dominican nun in 1974, standing before a Cesar Chavez social justice group dressed in blue jeans and huge Mexican earrings.

I am writing these pages in the coastal city of Vancouver where they have suffered the largest rainfall in the recorded history of the city. I have never appreciated before this what a deluge is.

The citizens of this city know it first hand. After many weeks of rain, they live a sort of depression, looking to the skies many times a day for signs of hope. They have had to remind themselves that it is not always raining. They have to think forward in hope that there will be sunshine again.

It has been also a summer of deluge in Manitoba, the mid-Western USA and parts of Europe. Deluge is more common than one thinks. Yet when it happens in one's own back yard, it seems as though it could only be happening here and now.

The Myth of the Flood

All these people should understand the Noah story. The absolute power of torrential rain is a reality that humans have always known and feared. We are helpless under its grip. We have no control over it. We feel as though we are in control of so many realities in life. Little by little we appreciate that, in reality, we are in control of very few.

The rain in the story of Noah lasted forty days and forty nights. Relentless rain. It is one of the "first stories" of the nomadic, tribal Hebrews. They had never known of any such storm. To be saved from death was an unforgettable event. They passed on this "myth" from one generation to the next to help their descendants bear up under any adversity.

God

The first character in this myth is God. Most of our popular theologies about God make him a good fellow. This story presents a face of God that is quite other.

The psycho-spiritual writer, Peter Pitzele, tells us about this God with a different face. He speaks of God in the following terms:

> *Here in the myth of the Flood is patriarchy's imagination of the other face of the Father. Not the creative father, not even the father of boundaries or prohibitions; here is the father of our childhood, choking with anger, sweeping the table clear of plates and glasses, hurling the telephone at Mother's head, shattering the mirror, raising his fist or the strap or whatever comes to hand. This is the father who can kill us—who has. History is full of his violence. He is the God of Cain, not just the God who opposes him. As men we may have imagined Him out there, but we know that He is in here. The Destroyer is another face of the Creator. The two-faced God does not seek in this myth to mediate or rectify His creation in any way. In the storm of his rage, he shows not the slightest sign of compassion.*

When God sees what humankind has done with the great gift of imagination (*yetser* is the Hebrew word used), which makes humans to be like him, he is distraught. His sadness turns to rage and his destructiveness reaches even beyond humankind. The whole of the created order is the victim of the chaos of this tyrannical God. This is a tragic story.

As I have travelled North America speaking to groups in transition, it is this same kind of attitude that is so often attributed to bosses, governments and to churches in the move though new, unimagined paradigm shifts. So many feel the teeth of some tyrannical tiger leading them to the brink. Generally the boss masquerades as benevolent, gracious, eager to help but, when push comes to shove, is ready to show this other face.

This is a good myth to help our generation live through

these times. Some are able to dance to their own drummer and accept change with some ease, while others go crazy with even the idea of change. But at this period of human history, when change is the name of the game, most of us have to opt for life or death over and over again.

As a civilization we have to do it on a grand scale for our common future. On a smaller scale, each of us has to opt for life over death almost daily. Death and static is always an option. In times of transition and radical change many choose that. I hope, like Noah, you decide to live.

Noah

Every child, woman and man faces incredible challenges. It is not only in the mature years that we have to face the unknown. As children, we have to learn the skills necessary to brave the storms. The story of Noah, however, portrays an old man (the story says six hundred years old!) facing new challenges. He had already lived a full and blessed life with his wife and children.

In this story, the Creator decided to begin a process of ultimate downsizing. He was upset with the wickedness of humankind and decided to make a new start. Noah was to be the manager of the change. He was to follow the instructions, build a suitable new structure and let God take care of the downsizing process. Noah was to put his energy into the project and the future.

Noah likely did not get some clear and sure signal from the Almighty that there was a flood coming (despite what the story tells us!). Chances are he followed a hunch, an inkling, about something that he sensed was going to happen. He likely listened to a dream, the skies, his wife. Who knows? Maybe God did speak to him. I doubt it. God has never spoken directly to me...yet.

From what the recorded story states, it appears there was nothing remarkable about Noah. He was old, he had a wife (whose name is never even mentioned), and children—Shem,

Ham and Japheth—who had wives (whose names are not mentioned, either). He somehow found more favour in the sight of the God than did any others. Were all the others so bad that they merited destruction?

As in so many stories of survival, the first requirement for success is readiness. Most of us are able to do that much. We live with expectations of disaster. I remember as a kid in grade school having bomb practice and crouching beneath our desks just in case the enemy struck. I'm still waiting! Most of us in our generation are waiting to be fired, waiting to be diagnosed with cancer, waiting to be divorced. Most of us live counting on storms to ruin our parade. So, in a very negative way, perhaps, we stand ready for danger.

The story doesn't tell us a thing about the character of the man or that of his entourage. He listened, organized and did it! The rest is history. He built the ark as prescribed, filled it with the appropriate inhabitants and lived it out. He is the symbol of the ultimate survivor—ready, willing and able.

He set sail from Point A and headed to Point ?. The story does not give us any indication of where he was to go. So, he left Point A and guessed. He was told to take two of each of the creatures, for continuity, and supplies for the journey—food for him and his family—but food, as well for all of the support team. It rained for forty days and forty nights, after which he floated for one hundred and fifty days. With no destination in mind, he had to manage the entire operation on faith. There was no map for the journey and no visible God to lead the way. He had to trust his hunches.

At the end of the deluge, once on terra firma, Noah lived out the rest of his life as a farmer. He lived with the intimate knowledge of the two faces of God. As a result he lived with a strong picture of loneliness and exile—two poles of anyone who has had to face the terror of major transition. It is not surprising that once on his own land, (the ultimate dream of the nomadic Jew), Noah drank wine made from the grapes of his land and got drunk.

Even though there had been a rainbow placed in the sky by the recovered God, as a sign that this destructive behaviour was finished once and for all, Noah still must have lived with the phantoms of the transition in the ark. It is not shocking that he would give in to the spirit of exhaustion and relief and get drunk.

Much like the creation story in Genesis 2, after Adam and Eve were dismissed from the Garden of Eden with all the shame that is implied in that, there still remained a loving God who assured clothing and compassion, just like the rainbow in this story. Bittersweet.

The other main character in the story is the ark. We will look at its significance in the next chapter. But first of all, let's move into your memory bank and see who some of your Noahs have been.

Heros We Know (Other Noahs)

Leonard Schuett

My dad, Leonard Schuett, died when I was two. Len was a strong, kind, gentle and loving man. He sold pianos and furniture. The family mythology has made him bigger than life. He was gentle yet strong; wise yet fun; diligent yet playful. There are many stories about his diligence—a major Alsatian virtue.

He would fill up the truck with mattresses on a Saturday morning, roam the countryside and sell them all to the farmers before the day was out. He would convince them, also, that they needed new chesterfields and side tables while he was making the rounds—the consummate salesman. He filled the store with people on Friday and Saturday nights when he would play the piano. People came from far and wide to hear Len play. I still meet old people on the street in my hometown who remember him at the piano.

One morning he came up from the store to the apartment above where we lived and complained of a headache. He lay down on the bed and said that he could not see. He was having a cerebral hemorrhage. He died that afternoon. Thirty-eight.

One day, as my uncles and I sat at the kitchen table to talk about my dad, their eyes welled with tears as they began to tell me about this wonderful man, whom I had never known except through stories. The image I carry with me, mainly through the stories, is alive and energy-giving. The few photos I have of him give me courage as I look at them. I wonder about him and even sometimes talk to him through them. I hardly knew him, yet I gain courage for my life through him.

When I was going through a rough time a few years ago, I visited his grave, lay on it and cried out to him that I needed him, to help me get through my transition. I needed his love, his energy, his stories. I shared my story with him and reminded him that he was responsible for my being here. He left me and I needed him. Interesting. I say I hardly knew him, yet, perhaps, in those few years, his energy invaded me and still animates me, enhanced by the stories and the hope of reunion with him one day.

James Morgan

James Morgan, one of my uncles, was a hero. He was one of the few in my life who, out loud, told me that I was good (even good looking). He worked at the reception desk of a very fashionable hotel in Toronto. He was loved and highly regarded by the people who frequented the hotel. Like most people who are "welcomers" in businesses, he became the face of the business. When the hotel wanted to downsize, they created a false "situation" and accused him. He was let go. He faced the humiliation and the uncertainty that comes along with dishonourable discharge. After that he suffered a heart attack.

My memory of him is that of a man who was in love with life. It was deeply humiliating for him to be out of work, but especially to be let go from an organization that he had taken such pride in serving. He had donned his tails and spats every day and gone to the hotel where he made everyone he greeted feel important and special. He had that great gift of hospitality. No one was made to feel cheap because they were not appropriately dressed. Uncle Jim made everybody feel like a king or queen. He knew everybody's name and almost everybody's story. He treated them all with dignity, respect and delight.

I remember him trying to bounce into a new state as he pulled his life together and worked at whatever he could, until he died...likely of a broken heart. However, he kept on with a smile for everyone, and was as hospitable as ever. His great gift for the world was that of hospitality. It didn't take a job for him to be the gift for people. He continued to be a welcomer until the day he died. To many he was never a hero. To me he was. His story helps me live mine.

Jim brought humour to the world. He was able to turn a story inside out and bring people to the point of tears from the laughter he provoked. How often I think of stories that he told, or phrases he used to make us giggle with delight. We still tell his stories whenever our family gets together. Jim is still with us—giving us courage for our days and nights.

Dorothy Day

Dorothy Day was a Noah who captured my imagination when I was nineteen. Dorothy was a zany woman who had a strong sense that every human has dignity. She was a strong, energetic American, who died a few years ago in her eighties. She engaged herself to the Communist Party in the United States. She saw it as a means of root reform within the American capitalist system. She dedicated herself to the cause, as did many young Americans in the forties.

In her growth she recognized that the Catholic Church in New York City was more engaged with the poor than was her Episcopal Church. So, she left the Episcopalians and joined the ranks of the Roman Catholics. She took her insights of Communism with her, and created the Catholic Worker Movement. She constantly struggled for justice—always ready

for the next moment. A major theme of her life was *dénouement*
—unclutteredness—and flexibility for the reign of God. She
and her radical disciples always lived on the edge so that the
next best step could easily be managed. No encumbrances...
magical insight for a rapidly changing age!

Her Russian-Canadian colleague, Baroness Catherine de
Hueck Doherty, caught the same spirit and took the "simplicity of life" model to northern Ontario. There, she began
Madonna House in Combermere, a lay community devoted to
working with the poor.

There are several Friendship Houses throughout the world
now—showing the homeless and disenfranchised that change
and happiness are possible. There is a community of Catholic
Workers who are just like her, in my former neighbourhood of
Parkdale.

Regina

One of my clients, Regina, was the eldest daughter in a
poor and large east coast fishing family. She had suffered sexual and emotional abuse from her father, her brothers and
their friends. Her mother was suicidal, and often the young
woman found her mother on the floor after an overdose. Of
course, it was up to Regina to look after the younger children
as well as to keep the household going.

When it came time for her to leave home, she chose a husband who would make her " feel at home." As a result, she married a man who was abusive. She lived with him as long as she
could bear it and eventually left with her two children. Regina
had no training to be in the world. She had only a high school
education.

It took a great amount of energy to leave the abusive relationship. But she did it. In the therapeutic process she learned
a new language. She began to read. Through all this she decided to go to the university. Today, she has finished her degree and has been at her new job for a few years. She is strong,
confident, proud and free.

When I told her a short time ago that she was one of my heroes, she blushed. When I told her what a good model she had been for her son and daughter—they grew a great deal from her strong choices—she conceded that she, indeed, was great! Victory.

Regina's son would often drop by my home for conversation. When I would ask him where his new ideas come from, he was quick to declare, "Oh, my Mom passed a book on to me that she had been reading."

That is how it is done. Regina had become a Noah. She served him fuel for the many transitions he would have to face in the years ahead. She gave him energy and hope because of her own journey and then supplied him with further resources so he could figure out his own way. Isn't that all we can do? Light the torch and pass it on. Then hope.

Paolo Freire

Paolo Freire, a Brazilian educator, worked with the poor, marginalized and illiterate *campasinos* in his country. His way of bringing about change in their lives was to introduce them to the Portuguese language, giving them the vocabulary that was needed to question the regime of the oppressors. He called this politicization of the poor *conscientization*. It was by learning the language of the rich that the poor could go after the tools they would need for their own liberation. Freire was a true Noah who enabled the masses to do the same.

Ursula Franklin

Ursula Franklin, professor emeritus at the University of Toronto, is another Noah. She has become one of the great radical (root) thinkers in Canada.

People feel helpless and powerless in this era of globalization. Local identity is lost. Mega-culture has taken over. The huge corporations have fled to the Third World. High unemployment has overwhelmed our social programs. More and more the poor are being abandoned. Health seems out of reach for the average citizen. The "little guy" feels lost.

She suggests that we act like earthworms, wriggle around, get together, fertilize the soil with ideas that are not on the official menu and resist the culture of compliance that is spread by the prescriptive technologies that define our world. This is an old woman talking to us—a hero. She practices what she preaches—wherever she can influence society. Her voice rises up in the press periodically and reminds us that we can change the world.

Hildegard Schmidt-Malo

Hildegard Schmidt-Malo was my psychiatrist when I was going through my forties passage. She was a wise, brave soul who was able to take a very broken young man and lead him with dignity through tears and fears into a new beginning. My first conversation with Hildegard was difficult for me. I had to admit that I needed help. That was tough for a man who went from early morning until early the next morning being "on call" for other people.

One of her first questions to me was, "Are you suicidal?" I was taken aback because I had always been the one to ask that kind of question.

"I don't think so," I responded. But before long, I was able to get words for what had been suicidal thoughts.

The journey I shared with Hildegard for a few years led me from darkest despair and fear into a new hope. She helped me tell my story. I had never told my whole story to anyone—not even to myself.

I cried non-stop for the first four sessions as I tried to express my thoughts. Later I realized that tears are often the first real words we get out in the process of healing.

As I told my story, bit by bit, she told me her story about coming to Canada as a young doctor and having to start out working as a cleaning lady in the hospitals where she would later work as a doctor. She shared her journey of escape and freedom with me. She told me about her feelings. They helped to validate mine. At that time I felt like I had no future, no person-hood. She made it very clear to me that I was someone and that I would be greater, yet.

Then she told me about her jump into psychiatry and her life as head of psychiatry at the Toronto Psychiatric Hospital on Queen Street. She invited me to lectures at that hospital and at the Clarke Institute of Psychiatry. She gave me books and articles to read as I continued to tell my story. She asked my opinion on cases she was dealing with.

Week after week she charted out my chronology as we explored every moment of my life up to that point. She responded as I told my story—often with anecdotes from her own life. I gained strength from her. We laughed little by little. We shared biscuits and cheese and tea and told more stories. Nothing was sterile. Nothing was uninteresting or unimportant.

When I was able to say that I felt I had no alternative but to leave the Order, she said to me, "I know. But you had to say it." Then she coached me into buying a piano, a bit of furniture— to ground me—and to create a bit of debt (she had a theory that a debt would force one to emerge from a pit). And soon I was able to take the next steps to freedom. It was through her stories, her laughter, her examples from others' lives, that I was able to get on my own ark and cross that sea.

Hildegard was also an artist. She brought me pieces of her art to experience. She shared with me some of her victories. These journeys into her other side encouraged my other sides. To know and experience that she had the ability to see and paint a tree, a flower—from the inside out— encouraged me to live my life again. Indeed, she was helping me uncover my life —from the inside out. Culture, spirituality and the ordinary were all woven into her healing.

When I took my first steps into the public as a performing musician, she and her dear husband, Frank, followed me. In fact, my first cummerbund and bow tie came from them. She was my *midwife* and helped me to birth my new self. And like good midwives, she remained interested in how the new baby was developing. I always felt her presence. I still do, even though she is dead now.

Later on, she invited me to join her in her practice because she valued my wisdom and recognized my healing ability. I shared an office with her until I was able to spread my own wings and fly away from her. Unfortunately, she died before I could tell her, in words, how important she was.

Jean Vanier

Institutions can become heroes as well—although it takes more health than most institutions can muster up.

Jean Vanier, a son of one of the Governors General of Canada, saw a need to deepen the sense of community for the world. He left the cloistered halls of the Dominicans' Le Saulchoir in Paris, and gathered together a group of mentally and physically handicapped people at a property outside Paris. These were considered marginalized people—unable to integrate into good society. Jean discovered they were good and blessed and could model true human values to society.

So Jean abandoned a life of honour and potential wealth and created a new ark for the world. There are now hundreds of his L'Arche communities throughout the world. He moved from one secure world into one of absolute instability—affording a life for the disenfranchised and ventured forth on an ark himself. Through his worldwide flotilla of arks, Jean and his friends are transforming society from the inside out.

Nicole Lettner-Howes

I received word a year or so ago that my cousin, Nicole, was living with breast cancer. Nicole had always been one of those zesty women who deliberately chose to live. She had been like that since her childhood. She married and had two boys and has established the happiest, healthiest home I have ever witnessed. In the past few years she resumed her teaching career but this time, rather than teaching French in schools, chose to work in the area of religious education in the city of Vancouver.

The cancer established itself in her system and the struggle began. With the process of chemotherapy and radiation becoming part of her regular regime, she was forced to retire from teaching.

At that point, I sensed a shift in her worldview. What to that point had been a domestic or local vision of life, expanded. Nicole became cosmic, timeless and very much rooted in the river of life. Her worldview moved into a new sphere. She seemed to see the domestic and local within a new, bigger context. She began to expand. She began to interact with the medical community, fighting for the rights of women with breast cancer, a struggle that went far beyond herself. She began to address national gatherings, to be involved politically for change. Change that she was invited to make (we can decide not to accept uninvited change) took her far beyond her own sphere and she began to affect the lives of others.

To watch this amazing woman take control of her days and nights was phenomenal. She is one of millions of women in the world who have battled this horrendous disease, but she is my cousin and therefore I pay attention. Nicole has been a source of enlightenment, spirituality and great insight for me. No longer was the far off and distant of major importance. What was most crucial became the now—to savour every moment, to hear every word, to cherish every heartbeat. She had always done that, but now there was new motivation.

Nicole died earlier this year. The private, quiet woman had become a beacon of hope. Her funeral was a very public event for someone who was so private for a long time. In so many ways, Nicole is still very much alive. I have a hunch that she is a Noah who died living—and because she opted to live in the moment with great vitality and zest, she will probably live on for quite a while. In the great scheme of things, I guess it does not really matter how long we live if we have lived even one moment to the fullest.

My Taxi Drivers

I am always impressed when I converse with anyone who has emigrated from one country to another. The heroic act of picking up and moving on is inspirational. Most of us in North America came from some woman and man who did just that, to get to this land. They somehow had to embrace the invisible and let it lead them on. For most of them, there was no road map, no rainbow, no assurance that all would be fine, just some hunch, an inkling that somehow they were being called to something new.

Sometimes they left their land because of an impending danger and risked all to come to a new place. Sometimes they just chose to begin all over again in a new place. Sometimes they risked the adventure because some new lover on this side of the ocean called them to come.

I always talk to my Toronto taxi drivers. They come from Ethiopia, Somalia, Turkey, Israel, Jamaica, Trinidad and Greece. So many of them are Noahs and give me strength with their stories of survival.

Often they tell me about their adventures of immigration to Canada. Often they have had to go first to Germany or England or Italy to get here. In the process, most of them learned new languages, new ways of living. For the most part, they have had to abandon their old careers, their families, their customs, even their dress, in order to arrive at this new point.

Once, when I entered a taxi a few years ago, I felt I was being welcomed by a prince. The driver, an Afghani, was sociable, articulate, calm and focused. I asked him where he came from. We chatted about his family. His wife and two children had come here, as well as his brother and his father. When I asked him how the transition was from Afghanistan, a war-torn land, to Canada, he began to tell me the true story.

His name was Rafig. He and his father escaped during the war and fled over the mountains, escaping gun shots and dogs. They eventually got to Canada via India and England. His brother and his wife followed shortly after with two small children. They succeeded in their escape as well and arrived in the east end of the city.

When I asked if his father were still alive, tears began to stream down his face. They had just nicely settled in their new home, everyone working and saving in order to start a new life here. He received word from his employer that there had been a fire in his home. Rafig rushed to the house to find that his wife was safe, but his father and two children were killed in the fire. We talked about his survival. He was a courageous man— a man with great faith and a deep hope.

He went on to say that his wife had lived in a deep depression after the fire. However, they decided to try to have other children. They have since given birth to two. Life is getting better every day. He was taking night courses, listening to public radio in order to stay current and to improve his English. I wanted to stay with that man for days and just talk. Unfortunately, I was leaving town for some time. I hope I encounter him again some day. He is a true Noah figure for me.

Would they go back? Most of them tell me that they could not. Some say that if they could, their children would not like it there. Many of them are stuck in a taxi. But others are using it as an ark to get to a new place. They go to night school, study through correspondence or through the Internet. Many of them listen to CBC, our public radio network, and educate themselves to current affairs and political interests. They are, in general, very smart people—proud, dignified and wise. All one has to do is invite them to talk. They love it!

What About You?

Who are your models for change—your Noahs? Who inspires you to risk new journeys? Who has shared with you the wisdom from their own process of becoming human beings?

- Your parents, your ancestors who dared leave the Old World to risk coming to North America?

- Your First Nations ancestors, who in the face of the European invasion of the Americas, kept the stories and rituals alive so that native ways could incarnate again and again?

- A teacher?

- Some mythical figure—Noah, Sarah, Judith, Jesus, Mary Magdalene, the Buddha, Mohammed, Martin Luther King, Terry Fox?

Most people I ask about their models quickly change the subject—embarrassed by the fact that they have no one to hinge their story onto. So many of us live in a kind of mythical poverty due to the silence of our elders who didn't value their own victories, or from a lack of ancient myths that serve as prototypes under which we live our days and nights.

I invite you to explore your photo albums, memories, yearbooks, bibles, literature and novels to see who has been an icon for you. Don't necessarily (or even) look for the famous. It could be a grandparent or a neighbour or a character in a play.

Call on them. Have reminders of them about—pictures, quotations, memorabilia. In a time of tempest we need all the voices we can muster.

Who are some of the women, men, children, animals who have been models for you in facing transition with courage, dignity and grace?

- What can you do to remember what they said and did? Pictures? Stories? Friends? Family gatherings?

- Have you ever shared with them the fact that they passed on energy for your journey—possibly without even knowing it? Why not tell them if they are still living? Why not talk to them if they are dead?

- Have you been a Noah in anyone else's life?

Things Every Noah
Ought to Know

Could be, who knows
There's something due, any day
I will know right away, soon as it shows.
It may come cannonballing down from the sky
Gleam in its eye, bright as a rose. Who knows?
It's only just out of reach, down the block, on the beach
under a tree...
I've got a feeling there's a miracle due, gonna come true, coming
to me...
Could it be, yes it could
Something's coming, something good, if I can wait
Something's coming, I don't know what it is,
but it is gonna be great...
—Leonard Bernstein and Stephen Sondheim, "Something's
Coming," West Side Story, 1959

E very one of us can become a Noah as we face whatever venture life calls us to face. Here are a few things we should be conscious of when it comes to creating the Ark(s) we will need to get through life.

Remember: Be crafty!

An Ark is a tool

When you go on a journey, it is the journey that is important—not the photos, not the carrier. They all serve to enhance the journey. They prolong the experience. But they are not *it*.

The type of Ark that you create to get you through turbulent times is important. Many people I have known have married themselves to their Arks. They have mistaken their therapy, a job, a relationship, their country, or some religious experience as being *it*, when these tools should have served as passages into something else.

How good it is when a client can say at the end of a series of sessions that he/she is strong enough to carry on without the other's help.

In his marvelous book, *If You Meet the Buddha on the Road, Kill Him*, Sheldon Kopp states:

> *…it is not astonishing that, though the patient enters therapy insisting that he wants to change, more often than not, what he really wants is to remain the same and get the therapist to make him feel better. His goal is to become a more effective neurotic, so*

that he may have what he wants without risking to get into any-
thing new. He prefers the security of known misery to the misery
of unfamiliar insecurity.

So many of the popular therapeutic approaches that have
been introduced in the past years—to help people deal with
their blockages—are good, effective and insightful. They each
contain seeds of wisdom that should help take a person from a
state of pain to some peace. They are tools for the journey.
They have been created by wise men and women who have
likely experienced the pain themselves. As a gift to the human
community they have rendered their tools for liberation acces-
sible to the masses. From gestalt to healing the child within, to
cognitive therapy, to *reiki*—each has shared an important
insight into the human adventure. And each addresses the
human from one viewpoint or another.

One approach might serve one personality well, while another serves another, or addresses one aspect of pain in the in-
dividual. They are all Arks. It is unfortunate that many clients
as well as therapists canonize these tools, and out of fear or
prejudice, never investigate new approaches. It is often looked
upon as betrayal to pass from one approach to another. This is
myopic thinking.

The same rings true in the religious community. I will
never forget sitting with a group of Muslims in Toronto, whom
I had addressed as their guest speaker. After the prayer service, we had gone to the home of the leader. The men were in
one room as the women scurried about preparing the feast
(veils drawn as they passed before us in the living room).

I leaned over to the leader and said, "Isn't it wonderful.
Ten years ago, I would have considered that *we* had the totality
of truth. How good it is to know that I have a glimpse of the
truth and you have a glimpse of the truth. How wonderful that
we can now share our glimpses and live in peace."

He, in turn, leaned over to me and said, "But *we* do possess
the totality of truth!" I didn't know how to respond politely.

This kind of thinking is also rampant in North American Christian religious communities where God becomes an addictive substance for many.

Religion can be a tool for accessing the divine, but it is not the only tool. Religious arrogance, I believe, grows from people mistaking religion for the relationship with the divine. The Ark becomes more important than the journey.

•   •   •

RECENTLY, I WAS IN SAN FRANCISCO and visited the amazing Episcopalian Grace Cathedral. Outside the cathedral and inside, the community has created a labyrinth. A labyrinth is a form of walking meditation that has its roots in many religious traditions. It invites one to follow a patterned walkway leading to a centre and back out again—a metaphor for the spiritual journey that we are on, as well as being a tool for personal transformation. The exterior labyrinth at Grace is embedded into concrete and is quite large. Several people can walk it at one time.

I struggled with the idea of wasting a half-hour of good tourist time to invest in the silly venture of walking along the paths of the labyrinth. I must admit I forgot that the word *silly* comes from the old Anglo Saxon word *selig*, which means "a blessing."

Under the blue sky and resplendent sun of the June afternoon, I began my journey, following the patterned walkway that would lead me to the centre and out again. On one level I was wasting time. On another level it became a very deep spiritual awakening for me.

It happened to be the anniversary of the day my mother had died, thirty-six years before, and I was in a state of mind that was predisposed to contemplativity. I was only nineteen when Mom died. At the time, I was preparing to enter the Dominican Priory in Saint-Hyacinthe, Quebec as a novice three weeks later. She died suddenly.

That anniversary always stirs up old memories in me, likely

because her death occurred at such a crucial time in my life. I was reflective and overflowing with deep feelings that day.

The journey through the twists and turns of the labyrinth was splendid. I reflected. I cried. I smiled. I thought about my various twists and turns throughout my life. What started as silly became, instead, a blessing for me.

I finally arrived at the centre of the labyrinth. I stopped and smelled the air, heavy with the fragrance of the lilies that lined the courtyard gardens of this holy place. I collected myself and said a strong *YES* to my life. I accepted the breakdowns and breakthroughs that had engineered me to that point—some sad, some desperate, most tremendous. Then I decided that I had to continue. This was an important journey for me.

For the remainder of the journey, I remembered in my mind, in my body and in my imagination, the scents, the images and the freedom that I experienced upon arriving at the centre and accepting my life. I simply had stopped and reaffirmed my story.

After that pause, I collected "my selves" and wanted to continue.

There was a woman, my age, on the same labyrinth, at the same time. I thought about her and her journey. She too embarked on her walk, likely doing much of what I had just done. Suddenly we were joined by a young girl who moved much more quickly than we did. She was being watched by her grandmother, who followed her with great delight in her eyes, knowing that the youngster was going to learn the path of enlightenment throughout her journey.

Then, a young man in his twenties also joined us. He was very thoughtful. I enjoyed watching his journey as he took each twist and turn and celebrated his arrival. Then he continued on out from the centre as the rest of us had done and left the cathedral close.

When I saw the young man a bit later, walking serenely down the hill, we exchanged knowing glances with each other.

We had both tasted the divine on our journey. The journey still continues.

I'll never forget the experience of arriving and enjoying the centre, but I also enjoyed the entire journey and all the reflections that went with it. We all walk some sort of labyrinth, whether it is a formal one or not. But to encounter another, whom you know has gone that way, creates a bond that we could ultimately have with every human being. We've all been there and back. We are not much different, one from another.

•   •   •

THE JOURNEY WAS THE IMPORTANT THING, the labyrinth the tool. I am amazed how many Internet links there are now on labyrinth. It is becoming more than an Ark in the lives of many and will likely replace the journey for some as they marry the labyrinth.

Most organizations exist to serve some present need considered important to the life of a community. It was really "Noah-like" to see the Sisters of Providence of Montreal build a new motherhouse in the late sixties with the sisters' rooms equipped with oxygen outlets. They had the insight to do this so that when all the sisters were gone, (because they were founded to do work that lay people now do), the building could be converted to a hospital.

In times of radical downsizing, rightsizing and the elimination of outdated structures, it is so often the case that people cling to old ways, buildings or laws that no longer serve, forgetting that they were created to meet some very important need at another point of history.

•   •   •

WHEN I WAS A YOUNG MAN I entered the monastery of the Preaching Friars—the Dominicans—in Quebec. We all wore cream coloured woollen habits that had survived the trip from 1216 to 1962. The habits needed to be washed, hand stretched and ironed. Some of the brothers worked hard in the laundry room to make sure we all looked good.

One of the early General Chapters of the Order, held at Oxford in the thirteenth century, had ruled that the brothers were to wear habits not of linen or silk but of wool. This was a poverty principle because at that time the undyed wool of the sheep was the least expensive. It was the fabric worn by the peasants. To dress like the people would enhance the message of the Gospel as the church had become rich and powerful and was a counter-witness to the simplicity of the message of Jesus of Nazareth.

By 1962, the white wool was extremely expensive. It was a fabric worn by the very rich. But the law was kept. The spirit and original purpose were lost.

Soon afterwards, the General Chapters suggested polyester. Now most of the brothers dress like the people they serve and only wear the original garb ceremonially.

How easy it is to get caught up in the Arks!

• • •

Created out of a need with the available tools

Most changes come about because the times have changed. Either we don't fit into our old skins, or we find new ways to face issues as they arise. My dear friend, and popular life coach, Rosalie Wysocki, often tells the story that she has learned...

The only way for a hard shelled lobster to grow is for it to shed its shell at regular intervals. When its body begins to feel cramped inside the shell, the lobster instinctively looks for a reasonably safe spot to rest, while the hard shell comes off, and the pink membrane, just inside, forms the basis of the next shell. But no matter where the lobster goes for this shedding process, it is very vulnerable. It can get tossed against a coral reef or eaten by a fish. In other words, a lobster has to risk its life in order to grow.

Each of us has the necessary tools within us to survive change, just like the lobster. But the first thing we have to learn is that truth. We have what we need. It is generally out of fear and ignorance that we do not access it.

In his book, *The Redesigned Forest*, Chris Maser talks about the process of facing major change:

> *Each new paradigm is built on a shift of insight, a quantum leap of intuition with only a modicum of hard, scientific data. But those clinging to the old paradigm demand irrefutable, scientific proof that change is needed. Such proof, of course, is not initially there in an ever-changing universe. The irony is that the old paradigm also began as the new, and also was challenged to prove change was necessary or even desirable. Time and human effort have proven the old paradigm to have been more right than its predecessor but still only partially right. So it is with the new paradigm: it too is more right than the old and eventually will be proven to be only partially right and in need of change.*

> *After 20 years as a research scientist, I know that a paradigm, any paradigm that has become comfortable has also become self-limiting. New data will not and cannot fit into the old paradigm because each paradigm is a carefully constructed impervious, rigid membrane of tradition that, like concrete, hardens with age and must periodically be broken, like the exoskeleton of an insect, if a new thought-form is to grow, a new vision is to move forward. This is incredibly difficult for those whose total belief system and personal identity is invested in the old paradigm. And those of us who subscribe to the new paradigm, whatever it may be, must understand and accept that a new paradigm can survive only because it is supported on the shoulders of preceding paradigms, all of which were at one time new, young and daring. There have been no failures on the part of those who adhere to the old paradigm, only changes that may have left them behind. And we who would replace the old paradigm must be wise enough to carry forward into the new that of*

*value from the old. The day will come when our "new" para-
digm also must perish of old age. May we therefore be merciful
with those who cling to opposing views and remember that in
their time they were right and on the cutting edge.*

To carry whatever is necessary for the future

I firmly believe that each of us has what is needed to survive
most ordinary change. We are both creative and resilient.
Sometimes we are asleep or frightened. No one of us is created
just for the present time. We are constantly going somewhere.
Our powerful imaginations move us on. Our blood flow never
stops until it stops. We are forever turned on. We are born and
we continue to grow constantly. I believe that we are equipped
never to stay static (although we might decide at a given
moment to live in the illusion of stasis). As we heal when we are
wounded, so we heal when we are forced to move on to a new
level of being.

Part of me hates change. Part of me wants to just sit still and
let the rest of the world go by. But then, along comes a phone
call, a virus, an unexpected visitor, a blizzard, and my whole
system is turned upside down. I adjust. I have never yet decided, in the end, to stay put.

I have had to face enormous hurdles, preceded by sleepless
nights and days, as I anticipated the impending doom. I have
stood before groups and proclaimed truths I was sure I'd be
stoned for. I dared confront evil that was even upheld by "holy
people." I've stood up for people who were despised because
of their stand on a particular subject. But I've done it. I've ventured on projects I thought would be risky and yet I've gone
forward. I've developed relationships with the enemy and become his or her friend. Partly, I think, because I dared to do it.
I had boundless goods within me to survive. I trust we all do.

I don't believe that a creature made for future is doomed to
stay where it last landed. The fact that we can fly beyond the
moon baffles me. My grandfather thought it was a big deal to

take the car from Walkerton to Toronto a few times a year. In his day, most of his townspeople did not even do that.

I know many people who never left Cape Breton Island to go to the mainland of Nova Scotia until someone had the insight to build a causeway. Now we can't keep them at home!

We can forge ahead. We might decide, however, not to.

It is easy to forget that the Ark is a temporary instrument

Arks are made for transitions. The Noah myth has Egyptian parallels. The word used in their rendition of a similar story equates *Ark* with *coffin*, the ultimate vessel for transition.

Once Arks have done their thing it is best to deconstruct them and reuse the useful parts. Or take pictures for the museum. In times of radical change, many people seem to get to the middle of the trip and decide that this isn't so bad after all. One can get used to the smell of the animal (and human) excrement that is being piled up in the bowels of the Ark. One can even get used to the inconveniences of the in-between.

Many are inclined to create leather bound, gold-edged editions of books that were meant to be in three-ring binders, for the interim. There is nothing wrong with interim tools but they must be respected as such. However, those who yearn for the good old times are inclined to canonize the sacred-but-painful in-between times as a new land.

Wait...an Ark is merely an Ark.

We are far from the old shore and have vague, distorted memories of what it was like

I lived in Florence from 1979 until 1980, just before I left the Dominican monastery in Canada. It was hell. Convento San Marco, the Dominican priory on via Cavour, was dark, dingy and isolating.

At that time I was unable to speak or understand Italian. No one in the community spoke English or French well enough to converse with me. It was 35-40°C most days. The summer I arrived there, the mosquitoes were as big as elephants. The divine office that we *chanted* so beautifully in Canada was *said*—fast, ugly and with no decorum—in Florence. Life in the Italian Church was formal, tasteless and legalistic. Most of the clergy were like museum curators. Even the Chianti we had to drink at table was poor quality. The food was excellent.

I loved and hated it all.

Then I returned to Canada. I was distraught by the way we lived. The streets seemed empty. The food was terrible. The people seemed too busy to live.

Little by little, I created a nostalgia for Italy. They knew how to live. They ate right! They became a beacon for me. I spent all my time in Little Italy *(Corso Italia)* in Toronto. I spoke Italian, daily. I wore only Italian clothing. I was truly a man without a land.

A few years later I returned to my beloved Italy. The trains were on strike, or they were late. People smoked. The food was not what I remembered it to be. It was December and it was cold in the monasteries. The towels were too thin and small. It seemed that every time I got into a queue for something or other, they would close the wicket and go for lunch as soon as I approached.

It is so easy to do that when we are in a time of transition. How often have I heard a widow talk about how wonderful Charlie was (once he was dead). How easy it is to forget the pain, the anger, the anxiety that surrounded him while he lived.

How easy it is to become a museum curator and avoid the present.

We can't yet see the new shore

One of the hardest things about change is that we are blind to what the next phase in our life might be. We live with the illusion that we could have prevented the uninvited change in the first place or prevented this transition time. To be in the in- between space is hard. But it is precisely in that in-between space, where we set down the roots for the future. To see the new shore could hinder us because it might not even be the best place for us. To have the future proclaimed as certain is a sure-fire way to static living.

• • •

GERARD WAS ALWAYS SURE that he would inherit a great deal of money once his dad died. His mom had died at an early age and he expected that his dad would follow suit because he also came from a family of early deaths, due to heart disease. But his dad just wouldn't die. Gerard had spent most of his life doodling with jobs and engagements. There always was going to be a better time.

By the time his dad did die, the money was used up. It was a very unfortunate shore to have concentrated on. Now Gerard was sixty—alone, angry and his real work had never happened. It was unfortunate that he postponed his living while awaiting another's dying.

• • •

AT THE TIME OF MY ORDINATION in 1968, I was living at St. Rose Priory in Dubuque, Iowa. One of my Canadian confreres wrote to me and told me that he didn't think I should be ordained because I was too "churchy" and not involved enough in social justice work. Perhaps he had some good points. However, it threw me into a tailspin and I walked around the monastery gardens with tears in my eyes and disbelief that anyone would find me unworthy for what I had always considered to be my path in life.

I began to think about myself. If the whole institution were to fall apart, who would I be in the world? It was a very important question. Was I just who I was because there was an institution that could direct my gifts for the world, or did I have them, regardless of any institution? As a boy in the sixties, I was never offered many alternatives.

Then I began to ruminate. Three words came up again and again. Poet—prophet—troubadour. That is who Kelly is!

It took me a few other breakdowns to make me realize that institutions were, by definition, too small for most people like me, and that my kind were a threat to the order in the Orders. It took me longer to realize that I didn't have to be part of anything, to be who I was to be, for my own pleasure and for the good of the world. I had limited myself by not exercising my imagination or my power. I had slipped into other people's paths, as being the only legitimate ones for me.

I did get ordained and spent thirteen years ministering as a Dominican. It was not where I would end up, but the experience served as a valid tool for me to be who I was to become for the world. It was a kind and generous organization and I loved the communities I lived in. But it was not enough.

However, in my case, it took an earth shattering breakdown that lasted several years, to convince my whole ecosystem that the shore I had embraced was not the final one for me. From 1977 through 1981, I was so systemically exhausted that I believe I was truly incapable of human acts even though I appeared to function normally. I had allowed myself to be stuck on a wrong shore and had anaesthetized myself from thinking of alternatives that would respect my soul.

I have worked with so many people over the past years who have allowed their lives to be sacrificed to the gods of fear, propriety and static. Often it took an earth-shattering event—a death, or loss (health, relationship, job)—to catapult them into new waters. Sometimes, they just died on the Ark, or worse yet, on the original shore.

We have to think of new alternatives even beyond the Ark if we are to survive

Often, in the middle of a change, we begin to hear new

messages. What we had begun to embrace as the new way to go, sometimes peters out. New insights can arrive once we have been able to break away from the former shore. Sometimes the in-between freedom, which we feared so much, begins to offer us new perspective on life and we like it. We have discovered that we could do without some of the security, material things or the prestige of the former life.

Or, on the other hand, we begin to see that what had pushed us out initially was no longer the reason to be in the new space. So we find it necessary to redesign the trip. Or new tools for the future emerge. Sometimes we shock ourselves.

Use your imagination! Create an image of who you could be in a million and one scenarios. Start to think beyond the confines of your own previous self-definition. Sometimes you don't think you have enough energy to do this. So do it with someone else. Get them to help you brainstorm the universe for answers to the questions. Or even have someone bombard you with questions. Most of the time you are not asking the right questions or enough questions. Do I have to? Could I go? What if I...? Do I dare...? Who would die if I...?

Most of us spend much of our lives stuck. To be in the middle of a tumultuous (or even calm) sea and not think of the next step is perilous and foolish.

Maybe the Ark we have chosen is sinking, stinking or too small. What is there on the Ark, or around it, that could serve me well to get to the next spot? Maybe I have to abandon it—even though it was the instrument I chose (or was chosen for me) to get to the new land. Maybe the new land won't accept Arks. Maybe the new technology has rendered Arks redundant. Maybe I have to retrain myself while I am on the Ark so as to be able to step onto a new land. Maybe the Ark is a blessing in that now, at last, I have time! Maybe I have to disassemble it and use its parts to create a new instrument for my salvation. Maybe there are enough winged fowl under there to be able to propel me forward. Who knows?

Collaborative thinking and learning from everybody on the Ark

There is a great reservoir of wisdom in all the passengers on any Ark. Each creature on the Ark has faced similar issues.

Last summer, I accosted a family of raccoons exploring our early summer grapevine. The mother was taking the children on a tour of what would be a delicious harvest table for them in late August. The little ones followed her and slithered down the vine, one by one.

I awoke from a deep sleep at 4:00 am to see who was making all the noise on the second floor deck. One little guy lagged behind. He was frightened. I wanted to scare them away. I stayed close by the little one as the mother eyed me and growled at me. The little guy went into the eaves and hid from me. Finally, she and the others went on their way and he stayed behind whimpering with fear. I felt cruel but did want to teach them a lesson (who was I kidding?). Later that morning, once this villain had disappeared, the baby must have been rescued or caught up with the others.

I tried to imagine what their thought process might have been in this dilemma. It was a good lesson for the little guy. I imagined him returning to the fold where the wisdom would be shared with the others about lagging behind. Would he return after his ordeal to pass on the survival wisdom to the rest of the family? Was the little one building up a repertory of stories to share with the next generation, a repertory he could call up for his own purposes throughout life? Could he now face the future with more zest, daring and wisdom than those who never had faced a similar crisis? Use your imagination!

Everyone on your Ark has a story. Everyone has survived to tell some tale. Everyone has developed skills for survival. Ask them about their tactics.

The animals in the Ark could also represent my own subconscious. I should train myself to listen to the many voices that carry on inside of me all the time, not only in my dream life, but in my waking hours, as well. Day dreams and night dreams are full of information for us. We are much more complex and multifaceted than we allow ourselves to believe. Our minds work overtime and all the time.

Look for the raven with the olive branch—together

Keep your eyes open. It is so easy to be discouraged and to see no way out. It is easy to be cranky and negative. It is easier to read the newspaper negatively when you are in pain. Try not to.

The old songs that were popular when I was a boy—*Put on a Happy Face, Whistle a Happy Tune, Smile Though Your Heart is Aching*—had some good wisdom in them, even though they could be construed as avoidance tactics. But it is better to try to turn things around internally.

I went through a tough time a few months ago. My personal code for retrieving my messages on the telephone said: "Kelly Walker." I changed it to: "Smile! God loves you!" Now when I retrieve my messages, I make myself smile. If there is a negative message awaiting me, I have converted myself to my own goodness and my own mystery before something negative hits. Just a little thing, but it helps me.

I can look to the skies for a storm cloud or I can look to the skies for a rainbow. I might get either, but if I'm predisposed to clouds, chances are that I'll get clouds. Invite others to be positive as well. Not pollyannish—positive!

It is important, as well, to try over and over again until peace comes. Be persistent. Noah had to send out the raven first, then the white dove twice, waiting seven days in between. He even took the dove onto his hand and put it back into the Ark for the seven days. Persistent and patient.

It Feels Like the Flu

Nostalgia: When you find the present tense, and the past perfect.

—*Abbi Sud*

When one door closes, another opens, but we often look so long and so regretfully upon the closed door that we do not see the one which has opened for us.

—*Alexander Graham Bell*

Times of transition are a normal part of every living organism. We and all of our parts are constantly in a passage from one moment to another. Somehow the myth of stability and sameness has taken on enormous proportions in most of our family and societal mythologies.

Most of us were taught to abhor change. Many of us were deeply ashamed each time we had to face some major transition along our journey. What a trauma it was for many of us, once we learned from life that we are constantly in flux. What a difficult stream of belief we have to go beyond, in a time when almost nothing around us has a stable future.

There are a number of things we should be aware of that go on in us internally when we are faced with a new beginning or a new ending.

Letting go is hard to do

Transition and change sometimes trigger grief. The same feelings emerge upon the loss of a job, the disappointment of an unsuccessful relationship, the discovery by others of some hidden secret, the letting go involved in an addictive behaviour, or the changing of a belief. These very differing realities all involve a passage from one behaviour or relationship to another. Even if we instigate the change ourselves, it is still a very difficult dance, to adjust to a new shade of living. We become so defined by the doing in our living that we take a shape that comes directly from it. Most of the time we underestimate how deeply we have been shaped by what we have been doing.

Almost with organic regularity we are called upon to make changes in our lives. Often these visitors come upon us from outside ourselves, sometimes from within. It is hard for us to understand that we are not always in control. We live with the general impression that we are in charge. Most of the time, we are, within the context of any given space in time. Then suddenly, out of the blue, it comes: a health crisis, a relationship "patch," a job termination, a rumour about us, an unexpected stranger, a new romance. We are thrown into a tizzy. We go into a series of disbeliefs and disorientations in our whole ecosystem.

These moments—sometimes magic, mostly tragic—throw us off kilter and invite us to reassess our identity. Letting go of old images we have held of ourselves is very hard to do. We have painted pictures of ourselves, perhaps very different from how others see us, and often have placed them in golden frames. We are invited (and we can refuse) to embrace new energy, new vision, new possibilities for incarnating our energy.

I know that I am inclined to hold on to old states of being. Embracing new reality is hard for me. It took my own breakdown in 1981 to convince me that I should abandon one form of life for another. My body had to tell me by crashing down all around me.

I refused to listen to my spirit in its sadness and depression. I refused to listen to the voices of others telling me that I must change. It took the collapse of my whole ecosystem to put the brakes on my boundary-less and selfish behaviour. Only after that crash would I stop.

As I grow older, I am not as attached to old identities, and have allowed more openness in my weave. For many this is not the case, and with age, the weave tightens and change is less acceptable.

•   •   •

BESSY HAD A HARD TIME getting over Fred's death. They had been together for fifty-three years. Lovers from their school days, they married at twenty, had four children and lived in the same town all their lives.

Fred had been sick a few times before he died but nothing incapacitated him. He had to slow down but was generally able to get around and do his chores. They had a good, loving and gentle relationship. They were together every day—always had been. Then a severe stroke took him.

It has been two years now. Bessy has not had an easy time. The grief overwhelmed her. She could not sleep. She had never slept alone more than a few nights in those fifty-some years. His vapour, his scent remained in the bed and she felt his presence/ absence.

When she would introduce herself, it took about one minute before she would identify herself as "my husband died." She had little identity beyond Fred. When her friends encouraged her to "get on with it," she told them to buzz off. It was to take time. She had to allow her whole system to reidentify itself. She had to learn to sleep, eat, think, recreate, pray, socialize and be by herself. That took time, new experiences and much patience.

Bessy had to decide to live herself. But first she had to get to the point where she wanted to want to live. That took many starts and restarts but as she says, "I got sick of being dead."

Now, day after day she is able to be the new person she has become. Her grieving did not allow her to be like another friend's mother. "The day Dad died, Mom got on the bus and has never got off." It took Bessy a few years to discover that there even was a bus! Now she's on it! Look out, world!

• • •

FORD HAD BEEN A POLICE OFFICER from the age of twenty. It was all he had ever wanted to be. In fact, he was, in the eyes of his friends, the world's best cop. He looked and acted the part. He had a whole collection of police stories, jokes and memorabilia. He travelled the globe and collected police stuff. He was popular, industrious and honoured among his peers.

He liked the money, the stability of the job and the respect that it gave him.

One of the things he most liked about policing was the community of friends he acquired from work. He was beloved by the fellow officers. He was fun. But he was as much beloved in the community, from the senior citizens he visited along the route to the people in the local doughnut shop where he had a coffee several times a day.

The police department offered an early retirement package. Ford was excited about it because it would offer him and his wife a chance to travel. He would also be able to find some little job to keep him busy and "off the streets," as he joked. But when the day arrived he went into collapse.

He was unable to accept the new identity. To be ordinary was an extraordinary challenge for someone who had always been in uniform and identifiable. He was unable to adjust to the new shape of his life. He missed the team, the camaraderie, the laughter, the stories and the adventure.

He came to me in a state of panic. Thin, restless, teary-eyed, disoriented, he spoke of suicide. He was unable to find meaning and joy in his life. He was unable to eat, sleep, or even play. His wife, who had been a good companion while he worked, became a presence stronger than he could endure. He had never really been a husband, but rather a roomer between jobs. Now a new identity became important. He didn't know how to relate.

It took a long time for his systems to recover. He was actually in a state of grief very similar to Bessy's. He had to refashion himself. So did his wife. He had to experiment with his life. He had no models for that and no practice.

The good news is that the suicide wish was temporary. Little by little he was able to come out of the depression and did create a new set of values and found a new identity. He eventually set up a little shop for repairing household appliances, which became the neighbourhood meeting place. He is now happy and fulfilled at fifty.

The shame of it all

Changes force us to leave hitherto secure land, to embrace a journey across a tempestuous sea in some unknown place. The in-between-time might be sacred, but initially it is devastating for most of us.

One of the most common feelings that arises upon leaving, or being forced to leave the shore, is shame. Shame is a feeling that is about unworthiness, uselessness and emptiness. It is invasive. As with jealousy, which is an emotion most of us are more familiar describing, we seem to be eaten by it. It seems so terrifying for people who were honourable, successful and strong to suddenly be overwhelmed by this feeling that invades from the bowels to the brain.

•   •   •

MAGGIE WAS AN OPERATING ROOM NURSE. She was one of the best in town. But when three hospitals merged into one in her city, she was let go. She had become so skilled at her work that she could have done it with her eyes closed. She would have been able to effect most surgeries herself. Now there were no jobs, neither part time nor full time for her to grab onto.

Forced into this exile, she began to eat. What was at the root of her sadness was reinforced by the dismissal, although it had been very honourable. She had been yelled at as a child by a mother who was obsessed with work. Maggie lived with a very deep inner script that proclaimed that without work one was useless. This most recent job loss aggravated the old wound and the grief was fueled by chips and chocolate. The circle of depressive behaviour began to deplete her of hope. The added weight reinforced her sense of uselessness and she grew into a deep hatred of herself.

If was only upon the crafty suggestion of another unemployed nurse that they pulled together a new business: offering post-operation counselling for patients and families who had to make major lifestyle adjustments because of illness.

With Marg's knowledge of psychology and Maggie's love

for and knowledge of medicine and her great gift of hospitality and compassion, they have been able to launch a very successful new business. They did reach the other shore.

Maggie had to be open to an idea from another, to value her own gifts and to dare try something new. However, the trip was fraught with fear, shame and self doubt. Perhaps it was in the pit of insecurity that the new ideas began to germinate. But they did. And Maggie and Marg were able to find happiness in their new world.

Claim your feelings

Freezing never succeeds in life. Only in ice cream. In any change process it is important to get the right words for what is really going on. All of those words are important. In a time of transition, we are more inclined to personalize everything.

- It is my fault.

- I'm stupid, fat, awkward...

- I'm not good enough...

- It's because I sinned...

- It's because I'm gay, Asian, French...

- It's because I'm not a woman or from a minority group...

Words are important. They put flesh on what goes on inside us. They solidify what invisibly invades us. Even to write them down, say them out loud to ourselves or to someone else brings them out into the open. Invisible demons seem much larger than they are. When they are described, they shrink!

And feelings are not right or wrong. They just ARE. But as long as they are bigger than we are, they can have very strong power over us.

Wobbly Bowels and All That

A recurring theme I hear when people are in transition is that they feel as though they have the flu. There is that familiar flutter at the back of the legs. Often it is accompanied by flu-like symptoms of diarrhea, nausea, sweats and dizziness. The threat of the new brings insecurity for many. It is good to know that this is common so you don't focus on it. Insecurity often brings on the flu symptoms. The body manifests what is going on inside. When your identity is shaky, your body will reflect that.

You must not forget that you are an ecosystem. No part of your system is independent of the whole. The healing process must always take that into consideration. Psychotherapy that disregards the body is likely doomed to failure.

Anger

Bessy said, "I'm not even an angry person but when Fred died I became a real grouch."

This is not uncommon in people who are in transition. Nothing is secure. All the old faithfuls, be they people, offices, desks, cities, are gone. Nothing seems safe. As a result many are inclined to lash out at whatever gets in their path. People who normally never let out a cry now rant and rave.

Often a period of transition will trigger angry feelings that were held back when all seemed right. These feelings might be about old incidents that had been stuffed into a dark place or feelings about ourselves that were overshadowed by good sentiments when all was calm. Self hatred often takes over and leads into dark depression about the present as well as about the past and future.

Sometimes an event that feels familiar can trigger rage that is unrelated to the present event. Some old shame might be triggered by a tone of voice, a smell, an insinuation, a place. In times of transition we are more susceptible to this kind of disjointed behaviour.

I was living in a low-grade depression awhile ago while I

was awaiting some medical results. I was unaware of the depression. I was tired and irritable, but it seemed like normal crustiness...until Morgan, our dog, ate the lamb chops that were thawing on the kitchen island in preparation for our supper.

I heard a crunching sound coming from the great room. I was upstairs in my study. Slowly, I slipped downstairs as I sensed that something was going on. When I saw no evidence on the great room carpet, but only those droopy eyes that can tell no lie, I said my usual NO! as the training book had suggested. He looked at me and yawned. Then out of me came a NO! from a very deep place I didn't know I had. It didn't scare Morgan. But it scared me.

What was really going on in me? Was I that angry with him? I could replace the lamb chops, after all. No, I was angry at other things that had nothing to do with Morgan. I stopped, controlled myself and figured it out.

Anger gets buried very deeply in our systems and often does not emerge for years until some other event releases the cork.

Depression

Loneliness goes hand in hand with depression. No one who has not been there can understand the dark hole one enters in a state of depression. When the sad feelings about the transition merge with the negative feelings for self, a profound fog envelops the person. For some people, this is a state they feel helpless to climb out of. Others see it as a temporary place.

It is interesting how, in the Noah myth, Noah goes into a state of collapse, even after the transition seemed to be well over. The truth is that the time after a transition is a period of reidentification. We are still in process—a work in progress. It takes time. There will generally be waves of depression for a period of time.

At the end of my major transition from the monastery to what we called the "real world," I thought I'd be settled by the end of the first year. At the end of the second year, I thought it would take another. It took about ten. I still sometimes have dreams of wearing the white robes of the Friars Preachers, almost twenty years after my departure.

Transitions take time. Even after we have new identities, the old ones never really abandon us. They are always on the Ark with us. And that's fine. They have made us to be who we are today. There is strength in that.

Disorientation

Grief brings with it insecurity and disorientation. What had previously given us direction is no longer present. Once again that could be a person, an institution, an object. We forget how dependent and interdependent we are. Some are also co-dependent on other realities. Some take their definition or orientation in the shadow of someone else. The more you consider yourself valid because of your relationship to someone else, the more insecure you will be when you have to live your life apart from that person or thing.

• • •

MELANIE WAS MARRIED TO JIM for twenty-six years. The last twenty years were shrouded in shame as Jim took to the bottle. She lived her days and nights in terror. She shielded the outside world from the fact of his drinking. She made excuses for him to the children, the family, the workplace—the world.

When Jim finally died, Melanie didn't know who she was. She didn't know how to be without looking after someone, lying, covering up, smiling. Her *raison d'être* had disappeared. She had forgotten how to be by herself. She was a child of an alcoholic, as well, and likely never knew how to be by herself without an external referent.

So, she started to take on causes and cases as she had done with Jim. She never made it to a new shore but decided to stay on an Ark. She continued to distract herself from her own being by finding her value and meaning in others. She spent the rest of her life enmeshing herself in everybody else's business and never was able to get down to her own business. Externally, she always seemed happy and energetic. Internally, she was a frightened little girl, afraid to let go of her many supports.

To date, she has never recovered. In fact, she functions like a dry drunk functions—one who would stop drinking, never bothering to do the required work for a new spirit to take flesh.

Frightened

Very few people live well with insecurity. Some master the art of portage. Many just stay in the rapids and get knocked around. The thought of portaging for long periods, not knowing where the calm will be again, camping on berries and bannock is frightening for most. It is frightening to be in between trapezes. It is hard to just hang there hoping against hope that another trapeze will come along! Who knows?

Most of us are ill prepared for change of any proportion. We were trained to be good, stable, employed, married, churched. To be out on our own is troublesome. We don't have the street smarts of the vagabond. We fear the loss of the simplest things upon which our lives have depended—a roof, showers, a pay cheque, security, a pension, a title, a uniform (even a three-piece suit), the clubs, a reputation, a citizenship.

Also, old abandonment scripts can be triggered when we are faced with leavings and new beginnings. Often the terror runs very deep and seems to come from nowhere. Sometimes the fear seems totally out of proportion and unrelated to the event at hand. But it comes from the darkest recesses of our memory, which are physical as well as mental, and can send us for a loop.

If this is all true in the daylight, it is magnified in the night. Even to have a bed partner does not eliminate the loneliness that is reinforced by the terror of fear. Our imaginations run wild when the lights are out and time is interminable.

Everybody Knows

When major redefinition takes place in us because of some change or another, we live with the sense that everybody knows about it. Some do. Most don't. In fact, most don't care. In so far as we feel guilty or inadequate in the transition, we believe that the insecurity is made visible.

I remember my first job after leaving the Order. I became an entertainer in a very classy piano lounge in the west end of Toronto. I was still wearing my invisible white robe, although I was bedecked in a black tuxedo every evening. The first week I was there an elderly woman came in and sat down at the piano bar. After a long drink, many cigarettes and a few songs from me, she proceeded to bang on the piano with the exclamation, "C'mon honey, speed it up! Do you think you're in church?"

I thought she knew. She didn't have a clue as to who I was or where I'd been. When you buy a red car, almost every car you see in the following weeks is red. So it is in transitional times. You are so obsessed with the new state and so infused with pain that you believe that's all you are.

NOT TRUE. You are in a very important transitional state and likely stronger than you've ever been in your life. You are working on every level of your being in readjusting and rebalancing. You might feel like hell, even look like hell at times, but you are likely very busy shaping yourself for the future, whether you know it or not!

No Damn Good

We have been so bred to be employed, have a definition, be in line, that when we are away from the pack we castigate ourselves. As I said above, we often feel awful during this time, as the old straight-line scripts haunt us. Even though some event outside ourselves caused the change in our path, we are inclined to blame ourselves for something or other.

I had a phone call a while back from a young priest who had been my student in seminary. He used to come visit me periodically to chat and to get some encouragement for his life.

After my last mid-life awakening, which led me to leave my marriage and to embrace a new life, he phoned and apologized for not being in touch.

He continued on to say that his absence was motivated by the fact that he was upset that he had been seeing me during that time when I was "mixed up." He was upset that he had sought solace from someone who was so confused.

I assured him that he had not sullied himself since I was not at all confused. Indeed, I was working things out in my own life at that time. I was in between trapezes. It was truly a great time to be with me—I had superb energy because of my transition.

At first, I had to fight against blaming myself for not being stable for those who depended on me. Now I thank God that they had access to someone who had opted to grow and change! I would hate to think that people would feel they should come to someone for help who was all done! I would rather seek counsel from someone I was certain was still working on his or her own life. To be all done is likely to be dead!

Food

Food either becomes a crutch during times of transition, or an enemy. It seems to depend on more than a predisposition for or against food. I've seen some people put on an enormous amount of weight during distressing times and others lose huge amounts of weight. They both seem to have something to do with giving up hope. One is a silent scream that leads one to disappear, while the other seems to be pushing the envelope of the cardiac system towards death.

These two tendencies are often complicated by either alcohol or drugs. Because of the low self esteem that often accompanies loss, we are predisposed to substances that start off as friends. As time goes on these old friends often don't work anymore and require bigger and bigger doses in order to have any effect. This even occurs with nice prescribed drugs.

Future-Less

The hopelessness that can accompany radical change is usually based on some old messages that have inscribed themselves into the soul of the person. It took some new event to reinforce the shame that was already deeply rooted in the person. Without a sense of self worth, we sink into the dark sad state of emptiness that has no issue.

For some, this feeling is so deeply rooted that it becomes almost impossible to overcome. Others, because they have felt loved and worthy in their life, are able to overcome this temporary state of hopelessness. Most people, however, who are faced with a radical uprooting in their life, experience it for some time.

I am always suspect of those who deny such feelings and claim joy, or who are inclined to thank the Lord for the pain. I never have been able to understand that attitude and believe this denial to be a sign of addictive behaviour.

I Can't Seem To Get Over It

Maybe you won't. But most do. It takes time. It might even take a long time. But, chances are, you'll get over it. Because most of us become obsessed with our pain in transitional times, it takes time and recovery to get on with life. It also takes new experiences of victory—even small ones, like getting out of bed, getting dressed, bothering to brush your hair, eating, taking a shower. The web of depression that surrounds us in these pits often blinds us to the fact that it wasn't always like this. There were good days. There have been other bad days.

It is so important to talk to people who are not zealots, people who are realistic about the possible duration of these transitions. Nothing is more enervating and disconcerting than a born-again recovering anyone. They have snap answers, instant formulae and seem to have perpetual gleams on their faces. Avoid them like the plague and seek out some brave old soul who knows that tough is tough is tough and who has a story to share, and some silent, compassionate support.

Partner(s)

Generally, the ones we love and live with are the ones who want us most to get on with life, and to pull out of this in-between time. Even though the times might be mystical and important in theory, they are a very difficult threat to our life partners. Sometimes, they are presented with a new image of us that they have never before experienced.

Many people engage in life with another because of some attribute—a demeanor, a social status, a position, a reputation, sexual energy. The relationship may have been built on some external characteristic of one partner. Once that special quality has been extricated from the picture, a new relationship might have to be created between the two. For some, this new person does not have the goods necessary to keep the picture perfect. Many couples break up under the strain of a major change.

As well, the one in transition might find that the person he or she was engaged to no longer has the goods to maintain a true relationship with the new reality. It is a time for most couples to take stock of what is left. Struggle and reidentification, on the other hand, can bring some couples closer together and help them both find new life in the adventure. But, alas, for so many it brings a death-blow to what might have been already shaky.

Sometimes a partner will take on a co-dependent attitude that makes it difficult for the other to breathe, without feeling enveloped or smothered by their worrying. They may push too hard, encouraging the other to get to the next step. Or they fail to understand the hole within which one tends to dwell in transition. It is hard on everyone involved. It is just hard!

Life as a couple requires intimacy for it to survive. That takes tremendous energy at all times. When one is in a state of transition there is no surplus of energy. To engage in meaningful emotional and sexual activity is nearly impossible for some. On the other hand, some seem to require sex at every instant in order to feel valid and loved. It is a difficult balance to achieve.

How important it is to realize that this can be an issue. It is not right or wrong. It is just what most go through in these desperate times. No one personality is the same as another and no two people will require the same attention. Some want lots. Others want none and isolate themselves.

I have known children to enter into a state of shame because dad was no longer the "this" or "that" who defined their lives as well as his. Their public face is spoiled in front of their friends. Their identity is strongly linked with the one that their family has worn.

Far From the Madding Crowd

Most of us go into a state of temporary isolation when we are faced with change. It is a time for hibernation (winterization). In my first book, *Loss of Soul: Burnout*, I talk about a temporal state that I call *Tardemah*. In the ancient Hebrew literature it was considered a time of transformation that happened in the inner tomb. A new creation can emerge after the deep, dark, tumultuous time. But not likely without it. In fact, Noah's Ark was considered a coffin in the rabbinical tradition of *midrash*. It is in this sacred in-between state that we fashion the next phase.

But that takes isolation. I remember seeing my mother (who died at the young age of forty-nine), lying in her coffin. For the first time in my life I realized that she was on an Ark— far away from my shore. I could not get to her. She was on her own. I realized then, that she often had been there—washing dishes on her own, knitting peacefully in the living room, silently wrapped in wonder and worry as she so often did during her many pregnancies that resulted in miscarriages.

Our lives are full of passages. And most of the time we need to be alone in them. Often it takes until mid-life for us to have the courage to be there—alone, afraid, wondering.

No one else seems able to be there with us. And it is important to make sure that they are not always there with us either because we have to develop language, insight and inner courage for the final journey in the coffin-Ark upon which we will embark at one moment of this phase of our existence.

It is difficult to embrace the solitude. It is not a popular place to be. Most people abhor it and so don't allow us to go there when we need to. There are, as well, myriad distractions —from the radio to food, from alcohol to sex. Relationships can invade our darkness and encourage pseudo-light when we really should be facing the dismal and dreary process of growth in the darkness.

Remember, it is in the dead of winter that the roots of the tree prepare for a new springtime.

The Deepest Pit Imaginable

It is in this inner pit that insight happens. This is what is supposed to happen in these passages. Not just out-sight but in-sight—new vision, new comprehension and new energy. But this creative thrust for the future generally comes to birth in long and hard hibernation. More often than not, one is tempted to give up and short circuit the time.

It is very important to let the winter linger. When it looks as though nothing is happening, it is happening—in sleep, in daydreams, in conversations, in conflicts, in reading, in chaos. But it is a pit—deep and unimaginable.

But We Always Did It That Way

One of the most vocal demons who tries to tempt us in our desert is the familiar old, "We always did it that way". It is insidious.

Convention plays into it. "It looks better. But you were more acceptable. You were successful. They all wanted one of you at the parties."

Whether the voices come from within or from external sources, they are powerful inhibitors to new beginnings. Whenever I have had to make huge changes, the phantoms arose. More often than not these phantoms are created by myself, propelling images of myself before me of how I thought I appeared or was perceived.

Sometimes people are vocal and dare tell us that they liked us better in the past. Sometimes, I've discovered, they are jealous of our ability to change. The most conservative among us detest change. Anyone else making a move in a new direction is a threat to their own security.

But now that you have faced your own truth and embraced new shores, you become a threat to the old order of things.

This is so hard to fight since most of us were raised to please, look good and not create waves. Waves are vital to life! Stagnancy produces death!

Mid-Life Clarification

The danger is not lest the soul should doubt whether there is any bread, but lest, by a lie, it should persuade itself it is not hungry.

—*Simone Weil*

I have met very few humans who have not stumbled into or been thrown into some kind of dark pit in the middle of life's journey. It seems to go with the territory. Those who claim that they have not endured a mid-life muddle are most likely in a sleep or in denial.

Mid-life is one of the first times that most humans are called upon to rightfully claim that which is theirs—their life! It is an invitation to be in charge of the few years that remain on this side of the curtain. Yet it is so foreign to most of us to be anything but victim to whatever arises, that few are prepared to take control. Some choose to avoid taking control of their own life and as a result, enter into addiction: work, alcohol, affairs, pornography, religion, worrying, control of others, perfectionism, or shopping. They decide to live an old life form rather than to embrace something more in keeping with the newly awakened giant within. Others decide to re-engage in what they had previously embraced—work, a relationship, ministry, whatever—and live it with new vigour.

Clarification seems the best term for this time—or maybe awakening. At times this awakening is brought on by a crisis—an affair, a firing, a death, or illness. Or it just comes with age. And often it provokes a crisis—uncertainty, fear, solitude, abandonment—in oneself and often in others as well. It is an opportunity for something new, either in fact or in visioning. It is a time when we can decide to see our lives either in decline or in progress.

Many people avoid the kind of inner promptings (sometimes screams) that invite change at this time of life. For some it is too terrifying to move beyond old boundaries. Some are frozen into old life forms because of culture, religion, family or societal scripts. Some have never been imaginative and so the kind of imagination that is required to have a zany adulthood is beyond their dreams. For some the door is opened because of desperation—the only way to survive is to create a future. Some need to be pushed out the door. There is nothing wrong with that.

This season can dawn on us at any time after about age thirty-five. But for most it appears on the horizon in the forties and fifties. Sometimes it appears earlier in the case of children of addicts who have had to suppress their childhoods.

This time of life is a most important phase of human growth. It is to be lived with savour because it is so rich. This period also prepares us for the final passage into death. Luther says that only one who has lived well can die well. Wouldn't it be best to consciously live all of the phases of life that are offered us? This phase is a great gift, presented to us so that we might willingly embrace living and enter into the joy and delight that aging can bring with it.

It is a time for radical assessing. At this stage the pages of our life seem to flip before us like a stream of traffic. The incidents that have caused ourselves or others pain and turmoil, seem to eclipse in scenes that appear present rather than past. It is sometimes overwhelming, as the scenes from the past re-incarnate and bring either pleasure or, more often than not, bring pain or shame. At times they haunt us. We question our motives, our sanity, our own actions. We are very prone, in this process, to condemn ourselves. It is easy to get stuck in self-critique.

It is, however, a good chance to own everything about ourselves. We can learn so many things from these scenes that sometimes haunt us in the night or in the moments of stillness that overcome our *busy-ness* every day. They are an opportunity for us to be reborn. We can stay in the past and let the feelings overwhelm us with guilt, sadness and fear, or we can choose to step forward into a new day. This uncovering is not just an unfortunate dip into the past, but rather, an opportunity to realize that we have lived beyond a certain event and perhaps even because of that event.

We can grow from our old mistakes. It is good to understand our past actions because they define us, to an extent. But it is good, then, to let the past go. We should try to remember that we have grown beyond these old ways. We can choose to use the learning for our future days and nights. Or we can let them torment us and remain stuck in old mud.

This is an important time to find some elder to assure us of forgiveness or to help us put our whole life into perspective. We need compassion from another at this stage of our life, mainly because we are so hard on ourselves as we do the inventories that force themselves upon us.

Sometimes the inventories are forced upon us by our children who begin to knit their own stories together. They come to us with blame or criticism about their upbringing or about our personal downfalls. For many this is unbearably hard. Or they come to us from those we have hurt in the past—either consciously or without realizing it. It is hard to forgive yourself for what many would consider "sin." It sometimes takes another human's voice, shoulder and tears to convince us that we are not so bad.

It can be a time, as well, for confronting some of the demons that have attacked us all our lives. Truth telling is extremely difficult, but it seems to be an easier thing to do at mid-life. There doesn't seem to be as much to lose. To realize that there are time limits from now till the end of life can produce inner strength we were previously unaware of.

Some of us are able to let go of some of the shadows of the past that invade our lives. However, some of us are surrounded by family or others who cannot let go of some event surrounding us that they have judged as evil.

At times, it is necessary to leave home and stay away from people, gatherings, cities, organizations that have vilified us. At other times, it requires our taking charge to allow family or old acquaintances to let go of their preconceptions of us. That might require a distinct separation or hiatus in the relationship, if dialogue is not possible. It is not healthy to maintain a relationship that continues to be toxic and breeds ill feeling. Sick is sick and should be avoided in honour of health.

This is a time, as well, for deep acts of love. The first one, which is the most difficult for most of us, is to ourselves. It is a time for radical self-embracing. A time to claim our bodies— just as they are—mesomorphic, endomorphic, scarred, or whatever. Much of our life is spent in discontentment with what we have been given. This is a time to acknowledge that this body, with all that it involves, has been with us and has been our eyes and arms for the world throughout many years. It is who we are and how we've been known and accepted for years. It represents us. It is a time for deep rebirthing of self.

I once witnessed two men side by side at Wreck Beach, a nude beach in Vancouver. One was a firm, muscular young blond in this early twenties. Juxtaposed was a much older man, likely in his eighties, body drooping towards the earth, which was calling him to return home. The picture was eloquent.

The young man was cocky and talking loudly to another about his out of body experiences on drugs and about many certainties, as only a twenty-year-old can proclaim. The old man just walked past and smiled —more vocal and wise by his silence. The old body had been there. The young body had much travelling to do to find the wisdom that only aging brings. It was a wonderful picture.

We must not bypass our aging bodies and treat them as unfortunate. They embody who we become. Wisdom dwells within them—in and through them.

We are a generation that has deified youth. This is sad because only the journey through the years can make us free. To be glued to youth can sap us of the energy necessary for the final phases of human life that should bring us delight and peace. To spend all of our energy on the various lifts that are needed to help us masquerade as youth is a distraction from the travels through the hills and valleys of aging that are part of our life—not some sad and unnecessary burden. As a result we might bypass aging, but we would miss out on one of the greatest journeys possible.

I once asked one of the old friars in the monastery in Quebec at what point in life he was sure he was to be a Dominican. He was in his nineties; I was twenty. He said, "I have been pretty sure since I was about eighty-three."

What wisdom to realize that living *is* the journey, not a practice! Life is to be enjoyed, embraced and tasted. This is not just a valley of tears to be endured in order to be perfectly happy in heaven. I would like to live my life knowing that I have lived it —regardless of what next life there might be offered me. I believe that anyone who postpones living for heaven will never find it.

Mid-life is a time, as well, for love beyond self. It is a time for ultimate stretching. To be compassionate, to become the other, to wear the same skin, to walk in the same moccasins is the essence of mature life. To be able to stand beside the different and embrace it for what it is. That is what brings us fullest joy. To stand beside the other and put ourselves above, and to pretend that we are better than everyone leads to division and arrogance. To place oneself within the story of the other leads to peace and friendliness.

It is also a time for sharing. Material things are here to be used or borrowed. That becomes clear to many as they simplify their lives. Material things can be shared with those in need. It is a time to be creative with whatever things we have. Wealth is not a sin. But it is to be shared in creative ways for the fullness of life on this earth. We are generally more able at mid-life to put material things into perspective. A generous heart creates joy and transforms society. A stingy heart produces ulcers both in the person and in the society off which it feeds.

Mid-life is a time for sharing wisdom. Stories are born to be told. There is nothing the next generation needs more than our stories. Generally, they become formulated at this time of life. I have known several people who have decided in their fifties to create collections of stories for their families. I wish my ancestors had passed on stories of their survival in their various migrations. Where did they really come from? What was it like? What were their fears? What sustained them?

It is also a time to share beliefs. For my generation, this is sometimes a period when old religious beliefs are resifted to discover that they offer some vibrant concepts and energy that undergird our lives. Often the politics of religion has blinded us to the energy true religion possesses. That energy and wisdom can be passed on—often very credibly—if it is done in context, without haughtiness and with serenity. Too often it is passed on in an arrogant or controlling manner. It is impossible for me to hear wisdom when it is forced on me as being imperative to my salvation.

It is a time to welcome others' stories without judgment. We are all trying to cope. Living is never easy. It is sometimes easier than at other times. Mid-life is a time to value others' stories of survival. It helps us put ours into perspective. I find reading autobiographies and biographies helpful. Or journals. There is wisdom to be learned from others' victories as well as from their failures.

I received a letter some weeks ago from a woman who had read my book, *Loss of Soul: Burnout*. She went into great detail about how the book had helped her in her darkest night. The word that kept leaping out from the page was wisdom. "Thank you for your wisdom."

I was quite embarrassed because I had never considered myself to be wise. Indeed, I wasn't old enough—not to mention smart enough. Then I phoned my friend, Sally, and shared the story with her.

"But you are wise," she said. Then she went on to tell me that wisdom was what I share to make a living.

When I told Ray about it, he also said, "I always told you that you were wise. Why don't you believe me?"

I suppose when the generation before us leaves, we do capture the wisdom that is needed for the next period of time. And it is ours to share. I am learning to delight in being wise and older. What a privilege it is to be asked to share what we have learned. It is important to discover ways to ensure that the stories get told to the younger ones. They need it and it is our greatest gift to give.

I hear so many people in my age group worrying about what they will leave their children. So seldom is their concern about anything but a financial legacy. That could be a good idea—although I have seen many "lives unlived" because they were depending on or waiting for someone else's money.

A better idea is to begin to leave the next generation energy for their future. That is done through story, through example, through art, books, recipes or faith. Money pales beside these real things. I want my grandchildren to remember someone who listened to them, who took time to be with them, who played with them, who shared stories and secrets.

I remember my old Uncle Jack Moore who took me into the bathroom of the apartment he shared with my Aunt Winifred in Florida. He told me that this was where he hid—you need a safe place to be alone (even when you're ninety-six, as he was)—and then told me that he had a secret.

The secret was that one could shave with petroleum jelly, that the jelly would sharpen the blade of the razor and at the same time lubricate the skin. He also suggested that I approach the manufacturer with this information and become wealthy.

I never did that. However, the image of that great old man stays alive in my mind. I am wealthy because of that. He and Aunt Win went dancing every week until they were very old. He died living! What a legacy!

How to Dance on the Ark

*If you always do
what you've always done
you'll always be
who you've always been*
—Sam Keen

*I don't regret the things I did.
It's the things I didn't do.*
—Evelyn Cotter

Arthur Murray set up dance schools around the world in order to teach ordinary people extraordinary steps for the dance floor. That was an important act during a time in the history of the world when people were shaken with war. Dancing kept millions of people out of despair and taught them more than fancy steps. It brought them together, pulled them out of themselves and led them into a new space and time. Here are a few steps that might help you join in the dance on the Ark as we live through these tremendous years.

You have to eat on the Ark

Ark time is a good time to reassess what kind of substances we fuel our bodies with. It is a time for seriously thought-out energy providers. Excellent energy is required for the kinds of decisions we have to make. We are mostly drawn to fatty, sweet, or salty high carbohydrate foods when we are in transition or down in the dumps. They satisfy us for a moment but soon the craving increases and little by little we dig ourselves into a body-depression. We forget that our bodies—not just our emotions—go into sad states.

These kinds of foods tend to lead to weight increase in most people. Bad feelings about our body image, combined with bad feelings about our mental and emotional state, can lead to severe depression.

This is an optimal time to exercise self will and change the ways we eat food. Think. Taste. Enjoy. This is not a time for deprivation (most of us feel deprived during transition times). But it is a good time for refocusing and realigning ourselves. It is a time to reassess the role food plays in our existence. Food can be a source of great energy and pleasure at the same time. Our body and spirit can rejoice in the tastes, textures and scents that we often missed out on in the normal times.

We are the first generation to have good vegetables all year. Where our ancestors were eating potatoes, parsnips, cabbage and salted meats, we are able to have fresh produce, meats and fish daily. Leafy, green vegetables, root vegetables, cabbage, broccoli, fruit and small portions (palm size) of meat and fish can give us excellent energy for the struggle.

Alcohol and caffeine should also be tempered at this time. If they have become addictive substances, they should be dealt with as such. But to use them and enjoy them with control is a good thing. Desserts should also be used sparingly but with pleasure. Don't waste your time on junk. If it is really rich and delicious, enjoy it now and again. To find a butter tart on an Ark is indeed a treat to be enjoyed. Forget the junk!

Eat little, often. You need all the energy you can get to make it through the dark nights of the soul. Spurts of energy are needed with regularity during the day rather than two or three major food binges. They take too much energy to digest, especially if eaten in the late evening. Think fuel. To remember that you are eating "little, lots" for the purpose of gaining excellent energy is a good reminder that you are in transition for a time—not as a life-choice. The food can remind you of that, if it is used rather than abused.

Keep your body flexible

I was on the train going from the airplane to the airport at the Denver International Airport a year ago. My arms were filled with briefcases, my winter coat and a suitcase. I could not grab onto one of the poles for balance. So I flexed my knees and made sure my body was flexible enough to counteract the jerk of the train as it came to an abrupt stop. It worked.

This is the image I hold for how we, as a generation, must

poise ourselves all day to face the abrupt jerks(ings) with which we are faced in the dance of change proposed by this new age. It is a good idea to practice the pose. I am more and more convinced that those who are stiff from the waist down are likely stiff from the waist up—including the head! That is not a good way to face the sort of atmosphere in which we live.

Everything that has a hinge in your body system should be flexed daily. Try to keep your knees flexed whenever you are standing. It is a good reminder of the flexibility you need if you are not going to get hurt in the maelstrom. We have to be as crafty as foxes and as swift as eagles. That takes practice—especially if you are, as an Irish nun friend of mine says, "on the north side of fifty." Tilt your pelvis, rotate your hips, flex your upper body and shoulders so as to keep limber.

It is vital to not forget your body in a time of change and transition. It is not servant to your mind. Your mind is in it as well. You will have more creative energy and hope if you pay attention to your body. Care for it. Bathe it. Rest it. Soothe it.

Find a massage therapist who can stimulate you. Shiatsu and acupuncture also can assure you of a constant and happy blood flow. The touch of another can bring great release, courage and pleasure.

Try to keep yourself sexually and emotionally stimulated. How lucky you would be to have a partner who could bring you peace and pleasure to reassure you that you are loved, loveable and good during times when you perhaps have a hard time believing any of that. In times of transition we are inclined to pull away from the lover. Try not to. Even force yourself to give in to the love of another. It will have its rewards for both of you. You need not dance alone.

If you are not living with someone, try to realize that you are in relationships with others. Go through your list of friends and consider who might be willing and able to comfort you. Ask them to. Most people are honoured when we dare ask for help—it could be to share a meal a week, go out together for a show, a walk, to shop, for a trip, for a massage, to sleep over.

If you are too timid to ask a friend, find a therapist (psycho, body, aroma, spiritual) who can support you through your life. Look in alternative newspapers for suggestions. Such people are trained to help others grow through transitions. Usually they have excellent energy and love to share. For most of them, this is more than a job, but rather, a calling. They are healers.

When I was in New York City a few weeks ago, I spotted an attractive woman—likely in her sixties—who was walking along and talking to someone. Because of the crowd, I could not decipher who was the recipient of such a conversation. When I broke through to her, I noticed that the friend was a little cocker spaniel. That dog, obviously, was her life companion at this time. I believe the dog listened.

Your friend could be a dog, a cat, fish, a perennial plant, which comes back every year and thrives on TLC, a bird who feeds regularly at the bird feeder.

In the past while, I have known of friends who maintain e-mail relationships. The other day, I heard a delightful story of two people who connected through the Internet and were planning to marry after having "related" for a few years. They had a conversation and then—from Europe to Canada— enfleshed the conversation.

In night's deep silence

A woman told me recently that she was going through menopause. She was able to sleep only about three hours a night. She said that she had resigned herself to the fact that it was going to be that way for awhile. I asked her did she read? She replied that she just lay there and waited and thought and waited. It is a good image for us in transitional times. Wait. Wonder. Let it go. We can waste so much precious energy fretting about the fact that we are not sleeping. Let go!

It is in the silence of the night that new thoughts occur. New dreams can formulate in those hours of darkness. The deep stillness can become an enemy if we define it as such. Or it can be a friend to play with. It is a time for deep imagination.

Dreams are also fertile fields for new possibilities. Pay attention to them. Take notes. Record the symbolic activity that goes on in the dark. It is as real as any other moment of your life. It is a very important source for inspiration and direction.

You might need someone to help you interpret your dreams. There are excellent dream analysts in our communities.

I used to fax mine to my therapist who would have a bit of time to spend on interpreting them before my session with him. It always amazed me how many hopeful symbols arose in the midst of deep despair about my future. I often got the courage for a future decision from the messages enfolded in the dreams: water running, blue skies, breezes, birds leading me on, flying. Sometimes I was able to confront, say NO, scream or venture forth, whereas in daylight I was frightened and depressed. You see, my dreams are me, as well.

One night I was dreaming about giving a concert. There were many people gathered around me. I was at the piano, performing *Nomad*, a song I wrote in the middle of the night— actually at three in the morning—just before my breakdown in 1981 (see appendix). In the dream, an old superior of mine entered the room and began to chat with people around him. I got up from the piano, went over to him and screamed (it is not my style to scream), "Shut up!"

I was so angry that I was unable to continue the concert. I awoke feeling incredibly empowered. I have a few authority challenges to face in the next while. What a gift to know that I can do it!

Change your energy

Brainstorm—bodystorm—soundstorm! Do anything you can to change your energy flow. We have so limited our existence to our heads in this century, we have forgotten that mind is in our whole system. So get up, move, dance, stretch. To put on some lively music and make yourself move to it could unleash all kinds of ideas about your life.

We play a theatre game in Sacred Acts, which is a performing arts school that my friends and playmates, Sally and Alexandra, create in the cities. We begin to walk about in a room, point to any object and call it by another name. It is an exercise that stretches us to use our imaginations. Try it. Then sit down and brainstorm on big paper. But first start by *bodystorming*. Move. Point. Stretch. Breathe. Move your imagination around. Then get new energy, ideas and courage for a new challenge. We get stuck...

I often invite people, as well, to explore their sounds. In a depression we tend to express in monotones. Make high and low sounds. Play with your voice. Groan and grumble and laugh and cry and scream and hum. Do whatever you can to get your inner sounds out. We generally limit ourselves to only a few possibilities.

We have a Nova Scotia Duck Tolling Retriever named Morgan. He makes a variety of sounds when he is around us. I have tried to imitate him. He gets excited when I do this. He has taught me that I can do something as simple as playing with my sounds to change my energy from sad to glad. It is free.

This will help pull you out of one space and move you into a bigger space. When we are frightened, we move into tiny spaces in order to hide from the enemies. We do this emotionally, as well, for protection from onslaught. But to expand one's arena changes the nature of the enemies. They get smaller as we get bigger. And so, exploring new possibilities within one's self is a very effective (and inexpensive) way to grow through tough times. *E*xplore, *ex*plode, *ex*hale, *ex*trovert. Don't hide and get smaller and smaller. That way, you'll suffocate when you could be breathing!

When I was in transition from the monastery, I found that when I was able to pull myself into a church for a service, the fact of singing a hymn yanked me up into a new hopeful time —even if the sermon was boring. I was also carried by others' voices when I had no song to sing. They sang for me and gave me breath to be able to join with them little by little.

I met a woman the other day who used to sit beside me during those months. She was going through a very difficult divorce at that time. When I told her how important her presence and her sounds had been to me in those dark night days, she stated that my being beside her was a great help to her, as well. When I began to get the courage to *ex*press my insides she was able to move into a new spiritual space. What was suppressed, once expressed little by little, led me out of depression. This was true for her, as well.

I cannot emphasize enough the importance of play and laughter during periods of transition. Even to watch funny videos, go to funny plays, read the funnies in the paper, be with funny people. Humour is an essential aspect of who we are. The slippery slide into "terminal seriousness"—a state into which most of us have been trained to exist—is indeed an aberration of our human nature. By definition, we humans play. Humour is not just a nice add-on—it is an essential aspect of humankind. "Terminal seriousness" is a disease to be treated. It is not the norm.

Try to find other humans who are willing to play with you —not to compete with you, as is so often the case in sports. But to play. To be with you. To go walking, running, shopping, loving, exploring, camping, to the cinema.

Be passionate

I was speaking at a conference in the north of Canada a few months ago. Sitting at table with me and three women was a man who looked as though he was suffering. He was glib, non-responsive and cynical. I wondered how I would endure him for a whole meal before I had to give my presentation. One of the women at the table who knew him asked him if he had started fishing yet this year. Suddenly, from within this deep dark and caustic cave emerged a daring young man—

even though he was in his sixties.

"Why, yes," he responded and continued to effervesce. I asked him what kind of fishing he did. He answered that it was fly fishing. I asked him if he had seen the film, *A River Runs Through It*. He began to leap out of his skin with enthusiasm as he said, "Oh, yes," and he proceeded to welcome me into his world.

He was a big shot in his industry. He was a huge success. He was passionate about something! I'm sure that the real fuel for his success in the industry is his great passion in the stream. They are related.

I have found that people who are passionate about something are generally able to cope in periods of transition. Their whole existence is not based on a job or a title. They live more than that. Their spirit is nourished by something alive.

Be assertive

It is hard when you are depressed to be assertive about anything. When you feel awful about yourself, you are inclined to let others lord it over you. It is a good time to work at saying yes (period) and no (period). That is a helpful way to claim your own rights and to keep the enemies at bay.

It is in saying yes and no in the most ordinary of circumstances that you can be assertive later where it really matters. Claim your own territory. If you really don't want to do something or to go somewhere, learn to say, "No, but thank you for asking."

If they persist in wanting to know why, decide whether or not you want to tell them the reasons. Work on telling the truth. This is, indeed, heavy learning for most of us. We've been programmed to lie, in order to make things look nice.

Pray

I was met by a friend at an airport several years ago. He

greeted me and then told me that his cancer had returned. He is a scientist. He made an odd request for him to make. "Will you pray for me, please?"

I asked him if he believed in all that. His response was scientific. "I believe if you send me your energy, you can change the metabolic structure of the disease in me."

I agreed. I told him that there were faithful women who met for morning prayer at our little Anglican parish in Bolton who could pray the hell out of any disease. I asked them to join me in the battle. He is still alive and well, years later.

Prayer has become such a political reality that at times when someone assures me that they are praying for me, I get scared because I fear it is a guerrilla tactic by some judgmental religious fundamentalist attempting to convert me to "the way." But to be gently supported by another in a time of trial is a great gift. Ask for it from friends. Some people are known for their powerful intercessions, for their great healing power. They are around. Use them.

I once asked a young man who phoned because he had to cancel his appointment with me if he would pray for a friend of mine who was dying. He choked and then said, "Yes."

The next day his mother phoned me and said how delighted the boy was with my request, but that he was at a loss as to what he was to do. This was the first time anyone had made such a request to him. He felt honoured that I would consider him because he was not, as he said, religious.

In my experience with human beings, I have come to believe that we are all religious. Most of us, in this time, just don't belong to some denomination. We are, I believe, one of the most spiritual generations to people the earth. The denominations have often forfeited spirituality for power and money. Most of this generation can see through that hypocrisy. We are very spiritual.

Transitions are very important times for us to piece ourselves together for ourselves. It is an important opportunity to situate oneself within the universe. What really is important?

What does this or that mean, anyway? It is a mystical time for discovering the significance of our lives, our relationships, our work.

Sometimes during a long period of transition, people make significant changes, enter into new lines of work, move, do things they had always dreamed about but never dared do, or they are able, at last, to abandon old scripts, relationships, values. To pray and to find oneself in unity with the entire universe can be a great source of inspiration and energy.

I have an icon of Christ in the great room of our house. When friends are in trouble and ask for prayers, I often am inclined to light a candle before the icon. In ancient times, this was a way for the pilgrim to prolong the visit before the icon. It helps me realize that I am sending energy from myself, as well as from the one in the icon to the person in trouble.

Most religions believe that we are linked both to those living at our time as well as to those who have lived before our time. In chronological time there is just a here and now. In *kairos* time, everything is now. That is the state we enter into in contemplative activity. That is where we may go in time of trouble. Why limit yourself to the here and now or to just those who are more or less available at this time? Stretch. It works for many people...

When the Irish writer, Samuel Beckett, wrote to his friend, Alan Schneider, he sent consolation in this way:

> *I know your sorrow and I know that for the likes of us there is no ease for the heart to be had from words of reason and that in the very assurance of sorrow's fading there is more sorrow. So I offer you only my deepest affectionate and compassionate thoughts and wish for you only that the strange thing may never fail you, whatever it is, that gives us the strength to live on and on with our wounds."*

Compassionate prayer is beyond reason. It helps.

Learn to live with less

Justin had lived in the lap of luxury for twenty years. His business was a great success. Then the crash of the eighties came. He was stuck. He was unable to divest himself of the properties he owned, since no one else had the money to buy them.

He came to visit me one day in his big Cadillac, which he was scarcely able to fill with gas. He said that he had defined himself by his possessions. So had his friends and family. He was now being choked by them. He was scared. Even though he had been raised in poverty, the son of immigrant working parents, he could not imagine himself surviving without his things. He wanted to commit suicide.

It took several years of being in this pit, unable to meet expenses and losing everything, to teach Justin that it was not necessary to have in order to be. From the desert of despair, he was able to understand that there are values more important than owning things. He began to treasure time, health, relationships, spirituality and his own creativity.

Justin was fortunate enough, as well, to meet another man who had survived the crash—an artist his own age. They were able to establish a strong and loving relationship. Justin learned to live all over again.

This time it was being and loving that grounded his life. He learned from a one bedroom apartment shared with his new life partner, that the *having* was of little true value if it did not have its roots in *being* and in relationship.

• • •

WHEN I WAS INTRODUCED TO BARB, I was told that she had a thousand intimate friends. She was gregarious, funny, generous and always on. I loved her energy. It was so good to be around her. Obviously, so did her friends love her. She threw great parties—her Boxing Day Party was *de rigueur* in the community. She was constantly in touch with everyone—sending cards for every occasion, visiting the hospital when someone was ill, always on the phone or e-mailing. She was quite over-weight but was always dressed to the nines and glamorous.

One February, after too many parties, too many gifts, too much food and drink and too many people, she crashed. She put on more weight, lost interest in her looks and sank into a very deep depression.

The dark time lasted for many months. People bothered with her for a few weeks until, little by little the phone stopped ringing, the cards stopped coming, the party seemed to be over. Because she didn't keep the dance going, the band stopped playing.

In the stillness of her dark night, she began to realize that there were only three or four real friends. She began to see that her biggest need—to be constantly with others—was not healthy. She had created a network of people who needed her to need them.

She changed. As she began to appreciate real intimacy with a few people, she was able to give up the many. Her life simpli-fied and little by little a joy she had never experienced blos-somed for her. She lives alone, but well. She has learned to live with less.

●   ●   ●

It IS GOOD, in these days of major shifts within our civiliza-tion, to learn to live with what is adequate for peace, joy and comfort. Excess will likely choke us in times of radical change. It would be good, as well, to model for our children, since they may not have the same material luxury in their lives that most of us have known.

No one is safe in this new age—no president, queen or bishop. The mighty tumble very easily from their thrones, as the world establishes new agendas for a new epoch. Those who were protected by institutions and power are no longer sure of a job next week.

We can be happy with very little. Most of the world is.

Claim your own story

Over the years, as I have been *midwife* to so many in their various passages, I have noted that they sometimes have a hard time moving on because of some chapter of their lives, some event that, for one reason or another, has invalidated them in their own mind.

I have never met a human yet who does not feel awful about something in the past. It could be anything from a physical handicap, to a sexual slip, to an abortion, to a criminal judgment—whatever. Sometimes they are private events and not known by anyone but ourselves. Sometimes somebody, somewhere was partner to it. Sometimes, they are even dead. But when we are in transition, these characters, either from inside us or outside us, appear in judgment.

At times, as well, these judges are alive and well. Many of them live in our families. They disallow us to take a next step because of their memories of some of our past steps that faltered, in their eyes.

Jesus of Nazareth talked about leaving your mother and father in order to inherit the reign of God. In many cases, it is necessary to leave home before you can take the next step for your own story. That is hard because it might involve being absent from the family reunions that all are expected to attend. Sometimes it is akin to the abused dining with the abuser time after time and never approaching the truth. In some cases, it might mean leaving town in order to establish your own freedom to be who you have become, not just despite some past event but, precisely, because of some past event. We grow. Often those around us don't and won't allow us to.

Every one of us is constantly being created by our stories. We have lived through them, integrated them into our character and moved on to the next chapter. They never stop happening. Just when we think the book has ended, a new chapter pops up. It is because of this that we become rich.

I know many spicy old humans who didn't become exciting "playing bingo and paying rent," as Rose sings in *Gypsy*. Their stories helped me. Their memories often made mine pale against them. But it was through their courage for the future that I was able to embrace my future with the same sort of courage.

Remember...

- No aspect of your life is invalid.

- You may have done some things that were inappropriate or that hurt others or yourself.

- That was then.

- This is now.

- You have become who you are through those acts.

- Let them go. They were *then*. This is *now*.

- Forgive yourself.

- Forgive the past.

- Get on with it!

Would You Like to Swing on a Star?

Would you like to swing on a star
Carry moonbeams home in a jar
And be better off than you are
Or would you rather be a mule?

A mule is an animal with long funny ears
Kicks up at anything he hears
His back is brawny but his brain is weak
He's just plain stupid with a stubborn streak
And by the way, if you hate to go to school,
You may grow up to be a mule.

Or would you like to swing on a star
Carry moonbeams home in a jar
And be better off than you are
Or would you rather be a pig?

A pig is an animal with dirt on his face
His shoes are a terrible disgrace
He has no manners when he eats his food
He's fat and lazy and extremely rude
But if you don't care a feather or a fig
You may grow up to be a pig.

Or would you like to swing on a star
Carry moonbeams home in a jar
And be better off than you are
Or would you rather be a fish?

A fish won't do anything but swim in a brook
He can't write his name or read a book
To fool the people is his only thought
And though he's slippery, he still gets caught
But then if that sort of life is what you wish
You may grow up to be a fish
A new kind of jumped-up slippery fish

And all the monkeys aren't in the zoo
Every day you might meet quite a few
So you see it's all up to you
You can be better than you are
You could be swingin' on a star
Gather moonbeams up in a jar?
You could be better off than you are...

—Swinging On A Star, Words by Johnny Burke,
Music by Jimmy Van Huesen, 1944

W ould you like to...? How wonderful invitations are. Sometimes they ask us to consider things for ourselves that we never thought possible. Most of us were never raised to venture a why not? Most of us were raised to think of ourselves as lowly, humble and possibly successful— but with strong hesitations. Americans were always better than we Canadians at thinking that they could be anything they wanted. We were raised to put on the brakes.

Transition times invite us to do this kind of inviting. Invite yourself to be successful. Invite yourself to be somebody. Success doesn't necessarily mean wealth but it could mean that, too. I have been taught to look upon wealth as a quasi evil. It could be. But I have also witnessed incredible philanthropy and generous hospitality by people who are successful AND wealthy. Not everyone is wealthy because they are crooked. Some are successful because they accepted a few invitations— even their own—to be somebody.

> *"Ask yourself, Josef: Have you consummated your life?"*
> *"You answer questions with questions, Friedrich!"*
> *"You ask questions to which you know the answer," Nietzsche countered.*
> *"If I knew the answer, why would I ask?"*
> *"To avoid knowing your own answer!"*
>
> *Breuer paused. He knew Neitzsche was right. He stopped resisting and turned his attention within. "Have I consummated my life? I have achieved a great deal, more than anyone could have expected of me. Material success, scientific achievement, family, children—but we've gone over all that before."*

"Still, Joseph, you avoid my question. Have you lived your life? Or been lived by it? Chosen it? Or did it choose you? Loved it? Or regretted it? That is what I mean when I ask whether you have consummated your life. Have you used it up? Remember that dream in which your father stood by helplessly praying while something calamitous was happening to his family? Are you not like him? So you not stand by helplessly, grieving for the life you never lived?"

"These questions—you know the answer! No, I've not chosen! No, I've not lived the life I've wanted! I've lived the life assigned me. I—the real I—have been encased in my life."

—*Irvin D. Yalom, When Nietzsche Wept*

When I left the monastery at forty years of age, I was in a deep, dark pit. When I had some success as an entertainer, I began to define myself as Kelly Walker—singer-songwriter and recording artist. Everything else I happened to do to make a living was incidental—public speaking, therapy, liturgical music and some teaching. The definition of myself I clung to was that of singer.

But I seldom got work as a singer. Most of my income came from being a therapist, speaker and liturgical musician.

I tried to get a well-known impresario to manage my musical career. After some months of hesitancy, he invited me downtown for a drink. He told me point blank: "You will never make your living as a singer. You are not Michael Bolton. You are too old and not sexy enough."

That stung! I had never thought of myself as an international sex symbol but I knew could sing and do have a certain *je ne sais quoi*. After the assault (at least it felt like one), he continued. "But you can do something that no one else in this country can do. Speak *and* sing. You have something to say. You have a great voice and a great capacity for communication. Do that and you will have enough money to be able to just do concerts when you want. You might even have a hit or two. I will help facilitate all this by introducing you to the man who can put the pieces together in your puzzle." He did. And it has worked.

I remember the conversation as if a steel blade had stabbed my heart. It was painful! However, it was good and important. His words echoed in my head for months. I had failed to recognize my true gifts. In fact, I will be able to do what he suggested until I am an old man, whereas my career as a singer would have been short-lived.

We can all swing on a star, but sometimes we are blinded to what the star could really look like because we are hooked onto a cloud.

Friedrich Nietzsche talks about "living the life assigned us." It has not been long for most of us since our ancestors left an old world that decreed place and class for all people. If you were not of the aristocracy, and most of our ancestors were not, you were doomed to stay in your place and never advance. Most of us are content living the life assigned to us until we awaken to the fact that, "I really always hated it." Most of the time it takes a breakdown or a firing to make us conscious of that.

It's not really a question of doing better, just being better. That's enough.

A time of transition can be a gift. It could come as the result of a job loss, a death, a divorce, a mental or physical breakdown. It has to be embraced in order for a gift to happen. The process could take a period of time. Generally we go through the grief stages that are so well known: denial, anger, bargaining, depression and, finally, acceptance and peace or resignation. But throughout that process we can come to embrace the Ark.

It is not a time to be meager and parsimonious. It is a time when we should be exploring all possibilities. Explore everything you ever dreamed of. In those dreams—which are from inside you—you have insights into what would most correspond with your soul's great work for the universe. Don't be afraid to be flamboyant in your explorations. Do not limit yourself! You are not just anybody. You are somebody. Don't forget that!

If you aim for a star you will likely get a star. If you aim for a treetop you will get a treetop. You must try to imagine a star.

•   •   •

MIKE CAME TO SEE ME just after he had suffered a car accident. He managed to get out of his car safely. He and a police officer were trying to help another young man who was trapped inside his car. While they were attending to him, a drunk driver sideswiped them both. Mike's legs were crushed. He had to have reconstructive surgery on his legs and was told that he might never walk again. He arrived at my office with a faint hope that he had a future. It was very faint.

I began to see that this young man had achieved a great deal in his twenty-five years. He had been able to start his own company, owned his own car, looked after his housing, had savings, travelled and had good and numerous friends. He had done fairly well in school but had never gone to university.

After the accident, however, the wind went out of his sails and he thought of himself as having no value. He also lived with the prospect of never walking again and spending the rest of his life as an invalid. That thought invalidated him in his own mind and he began to sink lower and lower. He isolated himself, began to lose hope in a future and became bitter.

Much of our time spent together was about sharing feelings. It took a great deal of energy on both our parts to get words about the feelings and more energy yet to get expressions for the feelings. Mike had been in control mode prior to the accident. He had stuffed his feelings about many things in order to accomplish and succeed. He had all the gizmos and little of the soul that he would need to propel himself out of the depression into a new start. Now the gizmos couldn't work. All that was left was Mike.

We began to explore the things that kept him locked up

within himself. They ranged from body image to dyslexia to addiction. When we began to take these issues apart, piece by piece, many things began to emerge.

In order to establish a secure body image, Mike had to express many previously stuffed phases. Hair was let grow. Ears were pierced, tie-dyed T-shirts became the uniform. Bracelets. Even his legs (which were quite mangled) were exposed. Little by little, he began to own his bodyworks. We shared stories about sex, explored his insecurities, refocused on the beauty of the beast and broke out of the self hatred that had been masked for such a long time by his doing.

Dyslexia. Although he had been raised in an upper class school system and had been allowed all sorts of academic freedom, Mike had never really addressed the issue of his dyslexia. He was ashamed of it. He covered it over by entering into fields where it didn't matter. But it always mattered to him. He had to skate around it in order to remain in his closet.

Then I suggested that he contact York University. They would allow him to tape his papers. They would allow him to be a university student and judge him on his abilities, not this particular handicap.

He went. He registered. He got his degree.

We addressed his addictions. Most people in this society have been bred to be addicts. Some addictions, such as work and success, are praised. He was losing himself in work, alcohol, busy-ness and success before the accident. Now he could neither do nor be any of that.

Withdrawal was tough. Along with the absence of these masks came an obscurity that was hard for him to stand. Now he was no one. The buzz that one can have about being clean had never occurred to him.

It was a long struggle to learn to rejoice in being alive and in some of the important realities of life. Tranquility, relationship, self knowledge. The process of detoxification was hard. We had to tell all the important stories of his life and discover what the roots of his addictive behaviour were. That cannot happen overnight. It takes time and effort. He did it.

We began to muse about the future. What could he possibly do? With a university degree and a major in Business Administration, many doors could open to him. He could speak. He is an extrovert. He is gregarious, affable and good looking. Why not explore that avenue? He began to take courses from Toastmasters. He was a success. His repertory of victories began to build. Perhaps one day he could take what he had learned through the accident and through the healing process and help others.

His new job requires that he pay attention to detail. He is forced to confront the challenge of dyslexia head on and not skate around it. He is no longer ashamed of the dyslexia and very openly talks about it with those around him.

Mike has had several operations. He can now walk. He has a university degree. He is in a good relationship. He has bought his own home. He has a good job, which he sees as a stepping stone to his future. It is only ten years later. It takes time. But you have to start somewhere.

How good it is today to hear him say that the accident was the best thing that ever happened to him. Did it take years out of his life? It took years out of one way of living, but gifted him with many more years to look forward to. Alive and well.

Life is always an option. Go for it!

A Star Gazing Page

1. In my wildest imagination, I have always wanted to…

_____

_____

_____

2. What is it in that wish that really grabs my attention?

_____

_____

_____

3. What did I do rather than the above as my life choice?

_____

_____

_____

4. What made me choose a career/relationship/city/lifestyle as a second best? _____

_____

_____

5. What keeps me from making new choices? _____

_____

_____

6. I resolve today that I will… _____

_____

_____

Or Would you Rather be a Fish?

*Eventually, all things merge into one, and a river
runs through it. The river was cut by the world's
great floods and runs over rocks from the basement of
time. On some of the rocks are timeless raindrops.
Under the rocks are the words, and some of the words
are theirs. I am haunted by the waters.*

—Norman Maclean, A River Runs Through It

N ot that there's anything wrong with being a fish. But if you could swing on a star, why limit yourself to the depths? Unless, of course, you have a fascination with marine life and the underworld. Perhaps, you could do both. Why not?

What keeps us from embracing the next possible success is, above all, is fear.

I thought it was important to end the book with these reflections because it is generally fear that keeps us from taking the final, most important steps towards freedom and inner peace. Even if our transitions put us in a state of deep pain, we can and must decide to move on if we are to acquire contentment and fulfillment. If we don't, we remain undead—that is, neither alive nor dead.

The main source of fear in change is "...the enemy out there." When my life circumstances pulled me out of one way of living into another, I was amazed at the enemies I created to keep me locked into an old and dangerous paradigm (for me, anyway). I had created thousands of people, in my mind, who would be absolutely devastated should I ever leave the ministry in the Church. I had imagined bishops who would be ever so angry at me. I had written a script that said I would never be able to make it in "the world." I had no talents, no savvy. I could never be in a relationship with anyone because I was not really loveable. I could never own anything, never be a success.

My soul had to push my whole ecosystem into spasm to tell me to get out of that space. It took a devastating breakdown to awaken me to the necessity of change. It took a breakdown of huge proportions to make me aware in my whole being that I had been living sad lies in order to get approval from myself and from others for who I was. It took an event bigger than myself to make me stop long enough to get the bearings I would need to save my soul. I was helpless—I became a vegetable for a long period of time—at least a year and a half. I pretended to be all right, but inside I was on the verge of death.

In a state of fear, our imagination turns to the most disastrous scenarios. We fear that our being is being wiped out. Change that is forced upon us is overwhelming and makes us feel weak. As a result, our perception about most of reality is bent out of shape. Enemies become huge. Our strength and value feel diminished.

I use the word "feel" because that feeling is real. "It's all in your mind!" we're told. You bet it is! And that is real. We just have to learn to cope with that reality. Because our mind is everywhere in our body system, we have to learn to convince our mind that the enemy has not got ultimate power over our being. No shaming, no blaming, no firing, no separating can destroy our being no matter how much it feels that way.

I was driving over the San Juan Mountains between Arizona and Colorado several years ago. It was the first time I had ever done mountain driving. I was wearing slip-on (and off) sandals. I had never experienced driving on top of the world. It felt to me that I was driving straight down the mountain. What was worse was that I felt I was on the verge of driving right off the road and flying down the mountain.

My feet perspired ever more profusely and I feared the sandals would slip off my wet feet. As a result I drove at ten kilometres an hour as angry truckers pursued me at a dangerous pace for them. They became enemies. The road became an enemy. The height became an enemy.

My perception became clouded. It was high, but safe. It was curvaceous, but I can steer well. It was everything I made it out to be. Old echoes came back of my stepfather telling me that I was no good at that sort of thing. Memories returned of the time when I was speeding along a gravel road with four other Dominican Friars in MacGregor, Iowa when we flew over the cliff (and dropped two feet—safely). Memories returned of when I failed my first driver's tests while studying in Dubuque, Iowa.

On the other hand, I forgot that I had never had an accident since 1968, that I had driven automatic, stick shift, trucks, station wagons, rental cars and never died. I forgot all that.

The next time. I will just do it! I have done my homework and know that I do not have to be small and afraid. I can be the strong furry giant that I am and just drive over those mountains.

More hints for a budding Noah

Get words for your demons
Once you have identified your sources of fear, you have power over them. As long as they are invisible and secretive they are omnipotent. Write about them. Talk to them. Talk to another about them. Describe them. Draw them. Demystify them. Put on music and dance with and around them. You lead! You are in charge of your being. No one can take it away from you—even though they may, in some way alter it.

Do a "what would happen if" journey
It is always better to be in charge of designing the future if some major change occurs. Use your creative imagination in walking through a new scenario.

•   •   •

WE THOUGHT OF BUYING A PARTICULAR new home awhile back. It was a beautiful home but somewhat poorly designed for our lifestyle. Many of the rooms were in the wrong place— even though they were most beautifully crafted.

We had to imagine how we would live in it. How would we greet guests? Where would we seat them once they arrived (the

living room and dining room were on the second floor, the
entrance and the "fireplace room" on the first). We opted out
of the deal. Our intuition was right. So we built what we
wanted.

•   •   •

I REMEMBER ASKING, "Who would I be if the whole Church
fell apart and I had to live outside a monastery?" Then I tried
to walk myself through it. I took off the white habit of the
Dominicans and imagined myself in an apartment or an ordinary house and living alone. I had lived in institutions from
the age of fifteen! I'm sure that because I had dared imagine it,
I could eventually do it.

Who would you count on for wisdom, counsel or support?

It is always good to have the card of an eligible elder, therapist or counsellor these days. No one should try to do the
dance of transition alone. That just doesn't make sense when
there are so many wonderful people around who could serve as
your midwife as you give birth to your next phase of growth.
Keep your eyes open at conferences, at parties. Who appeals to
you? What about them makes you think that you could share
your truth and your fears with them?

Most of us fear being made fun of

Our transitions will give fodder to the mean spiritedness of
a few. They cannot kill us. We are just a potential news item
until another "hot one" comes along.

•   •   •

SURROUND YOURSELF WITH A FEW FRIENDS who will love
you anyway, no matter what comes up in your life. I am so
grateful to a few friends who have stuck with me through my
passages. Several have told me after the fact that they knew I
was making the wrong decision here or there but felt that it was
out of their realm to stop me from doing what I, at that time,

believed to be right for me. Yet they stuck by me because they knew I had to experiment with my life.

Try to realize that all the passages in your life are sacred. They are your way of living out the dream that you are for the universe. And that dream likely requires you to go through your passages. Every story has a meaning. Yours, too.

• • •

CATHERINE OF SIENA, an Italian Dominican mystic of the 14th century, said that we were all created differently so that we could all help each other. Who knows whom you will meet who will need you to have lived through your passages—even the painful and messy ones.

Arm yourself with forgiveness

A person who is not willing to forgive cannot grow positively. To be stuck in hatred and contempt is to be stuck, indeed. Hatred disables. It creates a scum that covers everything in sight. It is important to try to let go of hatred and the arrogance that accompanies it. To forget that we are all capable of any mean-spirited gesture is to forget that we are all human. We can either soar or be destructive.

• • •

WHEN JESUS OF NAZARETH said that we are to forgive seventy times seven times, I believe he understood from his own life, that it often takes so many times to make forgiveness happen. To want to want to forgive is as far as some can get in the process, but it is at least living in the realm of forgiveness. To desire to have a heart rid of hatred and the fear that accompanies it is to be already half way there.

It is a good idea to ask someone who has the gift of forgiving to send you some of the energy that you need to change your heart.

To live in anger and resentment creates a huge stumbling block to venturing forth into creative waters. It uses up an enormous amount of energy in a negative and harmful direction. In times of transition we need all the energy we can muster up to move beyond the fear and anger that transitions generally bring with them.

• • •

SO, BE A FISH. Swing on a star, till the cows come home.

I asked my granddaughter what she wants to be when she grows up. She ventured inside herself, wrinkled her brow, then threw her head up in the air and proclaimed in a loud voice, "Everything."

I know, from my own experience that it is improbable that anyone will ever become "everything." But you can try to be almost everything. That requires the will at least to embrace "something." When you own one moment of your life, in a sense you own it all.

Nietzsche, one again, says, "To say yea to a single moment, is to say yea to the whole universe."

Noah built an Ark for his transition. He put into it all that he could muster up. He dared go on the journey. He had to make choices. He had to listen to the voices. He had to learn to dance with all the players. He even risked sending some of the players out to find the good news and test the shoreline.

You cannot succeed in the human journey if you are not prepared to risk. It is necessary to experiment with your whole being. You came into the world with unimaginable possibilities. You still have them, even if you are very old. There is no rule that says that you are defined once and for all. Your imagination has barely been tapped. Our imagination as a human community has scarcely been tapped. We have the goods for healing, for knowing, for communicating. We have only just scraped the surface.

This is not a time, in the history of the earth, for its creatures to hold back. Often we have held back out of fear or out of convention. We are living in the most important shift in the history of humankind. We either bravely swing from hitherto unknown stars, seeking answers, or we must delve down to the depths of the seas (and below) to understand the world that, so far, only the fishes have known.

This is all important for our survival. It starts with you doing it in your life. Now.

AN AFTERWORD
This Just In: July 25, 1999

M y dad died when he was thirty-eight, my mom at
forty-nine. When my life took a dramatic turn at
forty, from the monastery to playing piano in a bar, I had an
inkling that it wasn't all over then. I remember saying, at that
time, that if I failed to do anything about that crisis, I would
have to deal with it at fifty.

Well, as it turned out, I still had to deal with things at fifty
and around that time began to leave the marriage I had embraced at forty-five. When I had completed that break and began to formulate a new life, I had a hunch that there would be
something else around sixty.

I'm not there yet, but as I was in the last edit of this manu-
script, I was contacted by my physician who revealed to me
that my PSA count (prostate) had results that would suggest I
have further exploration done.

Since most men over fifty develop some prostate trouble, it
was a customary exploration to be performed. So I armed myself with mid-life courage and headed out to the Toronto Hospital. The medical team there announced that they could feel
nothing irregular, but that I should have a biopsy done at the
Princess Margaret Hospital just to be sure. After that, I returned home to await the regular news that, as usual, nothing
was wrong and that I should just lose some weight and walk
more.

In late July the phone rang. It was Ann from Doctor Stewart's office. There were six biopsies taken (it felt like twelve) and of them five were fine. One showed traces of cancer. I thanked her for being so gracious as to phone me (I had asked that she might), hung up the receiver and made it into the chesterfield in the great room of our home. I started to cry. I was alone. And I was dying!

It is amazing how quickly we can do an inventory of our life. In a very few minutes, I reviewed all my life. I tripped on a few images, but was relentless in my inventory. The tears danced with the guilt and fear and some of the delight of my life.

I sobbed like a baby as I recalled that at birth I was smaller than my mom's hand, that I had been kept in a shoe box in the oven door, bathed with olive oil and fed with an eye dropper. My dad had died when I was two and a half. We moved. My mom remarried. We moved again. I went to three schools in Grade One. We moved again. And again. My little brother was born. I went away and entered the Christian Brothers at fifteen. I left. I went away to university. I entered the Dominican Monastery at twenty. I left at forty. I married at forty-five. I left at fifty-two. I settled down at last at fifty-three. I was to have my fifty-eighth birthday in August. Would I be alive for it? Was everything a failure? Could I stick with anything? Who had I hurt? What good was it all? Had I spent all my life running? The tears and fear wove a web of despair as I looked to a future of death. Dead is dead.

Then I pulled myself together and reminded myself that I had also been a success. I had been a good person. I had helped thousands of people. I was a happy soul with a positive outlook on life. Even on death. This news did not mean that I was going to die. I had told all kinds of people that cancer does not mean death. But Nicole had just died. Ron died of cancer. And Richard. And we just buried Peter. But Mark is still alive. Art is alive. Eileen is still here and well. Mary, too.

Then God. What about him? I told everyone that he would be faithful and never let us go. We are carved into the palm of his hand. Why was he abandoning me now? Do I even believe in God? I hadn't been to church for some time. I hadn't been to confession in years. Would God understand my alienation from the institutional church? Did all of that matter? Did my belief in another life hold water? Was it rooted in deep faith or was it an *X-Files* inkling?

My mind wandered to all my loved ones. Would they be all right? Should I tell anyone? Do I have enough insurance to look after my family? Have I left anything to anybody? Money? Heritage? I haven't finished this book yet. The new CD. Will I be able to make a living? How long will I live? Will we be able to support my dying? Do I have to be a burden on everyone and ruin their lives with all this?

Will there be pain? Will I become impotent and incontinent. They told me these could result from prostate cancer. I was supposed to have been impotent until I left the monastery. My heart was never really celibate. I tried. Now I would have to be. Damn. Can I stand up and talk or sing to people if I am incontinent? Am I a loser? Why not just die now and get it over with. Why the waiting?

The greatest pain will be leaving my loved ones. I have such a great life. A great partner—loving, compassionate and generous. I have great children—my own and all the ones I've nurtured through my life. Morgan. Will our little dog remember me? Will anyone remember me? Has my work been significant? Did I help anyone in any depth?

And on it went—tears mixed with self-doubt, self- condemnation, fear and trepidation. Pure terror.

Then I awoke to the realization that Ann had said that there was 5% of one of the biopsies that was cancerous— 5%! Not all of it or all of them—5%.

You are not going to die. You are likely highly curable. You have the best doctors, the best support systems, the best lifestyle possible to rebalance your system. You will likely die of something else before you die of prostate cancer. Most men die *with* it. Very few die *from* it. At least that's what the literature says. You have to choose how to deal with it: radiation, prostatectomy—it's up to you.

Little by little I cooled down. Then the waves began again. Finally I called my partner. I said it OUT LOUD. I HAVE CANCER! We talked. I got the best support there that I could imagine. I decided to call my two friends who had lived with breast cancer for the past number of years. They listened. They shared. My hope was increased.

Later that day, I sat down at my desk and hooked up to the Internet. I keyed in prostate cancer. Miles of information appeared, from data to personal stories about prognosis, about feelings, about treatment and cure. I couldn't believe it. Then I e-mailed the friends who shared e-mail with me and asked for support, prayers, energy, love, whatever they had to offer. Within a few hours, there was encouragement, tears, stories, contacts, recipes and remedies. Most of them were men. Men ready to share and be open. The women were great. I expected that. But the men showed a kind of compassion that amazed me.

Another new friend found out and sent me a book that helped him with his prostate cancer journey. He wanted me to know that I could call at any time and get support.

A great man who had been my therapist during a difficult period, heard that I had prostate cancer and phoned to tell me that he had also had it, been treated and was safely recovered. He said that he would be very happy to be with me during any of the journey—even to accompany me to the hospital.

What was death a few hours previous had now become a new form of living. I decided to be very open and honest with everyone in my circle of friends. I decided that I would initiate conversation. I am in charge of this process. The terror of the first morning began to fade.

Until night. Then all the phantoms were let loose. I imagined my funeral, my burial or my cremation. I wondered where it would be. Who would come? What could they say about me? What would my beloved Ash Croft be for my partner and dog without me? Would someone take my place? I hoped so and at the same time didn't want anyone else there. What about my manager? His living also depends upon mine. What about...? What about...? What about...?

I went for a walk in the dark. I cried. I looked at the stars and imagined myself somewhere out there. I talked to my mom and dad, dead for such a long time. I asked for peace. I even asked God, who seemed very invisible. I prayed the Our Father. And meant it. I walked and wondered. I returned to bed and waited for dawn. I felt safe there. But scared.

That old nun who said to me, "When the Lord sends you tribulations, he expects you to tribulate," really knew what she was talking about. And the text from Dante's *Commedia: nel mezzo del cammin di nostra vita*...in the middle of the road of my life, I awoke in a dark woods where the true way was wholly lost—also knew what he was talking about. I wonder what his cancer was.

But the sun did shine the next days. And the reality that I am mortal is now firmly implanted into my consciousness. I know that I will live for a time. And then I'll die. However, in the time between now and then—which could be thirty years—I hope that this chaos has presented me with the Arks I need to journey as a brave Noah from here to there.

BIBLIOGRAPHY
Suggested Reading

Alter, Robert. *Genesis, Translation and Commentary*. New York: W.W. Norton, 1996.

Anderson, Walter Truett. *Reality Isn't What It Used To Be*, Theatrical Politics, Ready-to-Wear Religion, Global Myths, Primitive Chic, and Other Wonders of the Postmodern World.. San Francisco, Harper, 1990.

Arbuckle, G.A. *Earthing the Gospel: An Inculturation Handbook for the Pastoral Worker.* Maryknoll, NY: Orbis Books, 1990.

—. *Out of Chaos: Refounding of Religious Congregations*. New York: Paulist Press, 1988.

—. *Change, Grief and Renewal in the Church*. Westminster, MD: Christian Classics, 1991.

Armstrong, Karen. *In the Beginning, A New Interpretation of Genesis*. New York: Alfred A. Knopf, 1996.

Bernstein, Leonard, and Stephen Sondheim. *West Side Story*. New York:, 1959.

Blackburn, Julia. *Daisy Bates in the Desert, A Woman's Life among the Aborigines*. New York: Pantheon Books, 1994.

Boldt, Laurence C. *Zen and the Art of Making a Living, A Practical Guide to Creative Career Design*. New York: Arkana, 1991.

—. *How to Find the Work You Love*. New York: Arkana, 1996.

Booth, Leo. *When God Becomes a Drug*. Long Beach: SCP Limited, 1998.

Bridges, William. *Transitions, Making Sense of Life's Changes*. Reading, MA: Addison-Wesley Publishing Co., 1980.

—. *Managing Transitions, Making the Most of Change*. Reading, MA: Addison-Wesley Publishing Co., 1991.

—. *Surviving Corporate Transition: Rational Management in a World of Mergers, Layoffs, Start-ups, Takeovers, Divestitures, Deregulation and New Technologies*. New York: Doubleday, 1988.

Capacchione, Lucia. *The Power of Your Other Hand, A Course in Channeling the Inner Wisdom of the Right Brain*. North Hollywood: Newcastle, 1988.

Crossan, John Dominic. *Jesus, A Revolutionary Biography*. San Francisco: Harper, 1994.

Csikszentimihalyi, Mihaly. *Finding Flow, the Psychology of Engagement with Everyday Life*. New York: Harper Collins Basic Books, 1997.

Cohn, Norman. *Noah's Flood: The Genesis Story in Western Thought*. New Haven: Yale University Press, 1996.

—. *The Pursuit of the Millennium: Revolutionary Millennarians and Mystical Anarchists of the Middle Ages*. London: Palladin (3rd Edition 1970 [1957]).

—. *Cosmos, Chaos and the World to Come: The Ancient Roots of Apocalyptic Faith*. New Haven: Yale University Press, 1993.

Conroy, Pat. *The Great Santini*. New York, Bantam, 1976.

—. *The Prince of Tides*. New York: Bantam, 1986.

Ferder, Fran, and John Heagle. *Partnership. Men and Women in Ministry*. Notre Dame, IN: Ave Maria Press, 1989.

Findley, Timothy. *Not Wanted on the Voyage*. Toronto: Penguin Books, 1984.

Fokkelman, J.P. *Narrative Art in Genesis: Specimens of Stylistic and Structural Analysis*. Essen: Van Gorcum, 1975.

Fox, Everett. *The Five Books of Moses. A New Translation with Introductions, Commentary and Notes*. New York: Schocken, 1995.

Gullette, Margaret Morganroth. *Declining to Decline: Cultural Combat and the Politics of Midlife*. Charlottesville: University Press of Virginia, 1997.

Halpin, Marlene. *Forgiving, Present Perfect*. Dubuque: W.C. Brown Co., 1987.

Harrikson, Troon, and Eugenie Fernandes. *Lavender Moon*. Toronto: Annick Press, 1997.*

Hamel, G., and C.K. Prahalad. "Strategic Intent," in *Harvard Business Review*. Vol. 67, No. 3, 1989, pp. 63-76.

Hamer, M., and J. Champy. *The Reengineering Corporation*. New York: Harper Collins, 1994.

Heilbrun, Carolyn. *The Last Gift of Time: Life Beyond Sixty*. New York: Dial Press, 1997.

Kabat-Zinn, John. *Full Catastrophe Living*. New York: Dell, 1990.

Kaufman, Gershin. *Shame: The Power of Caring*. Rochester, VT: Shenkman, 1985.

Keen, Sam. *Fire In the Belly, On Being a Man*. New York: Bantam Books, 1991.

—. *Inward Bound, Exploring the Geography of Your Emotions*. New York: Bantam Books, 1992.

Kopp, Sheldon. *If You Meet the Buddha On the Road, Kill Him! The Pilgrimage of Psychotherapy Patients*. New York: Bantam Books, 1972.

Kriegel, Robert J., and Louis Patler. *If It Ain't Broke, Break It! And Other Unconventional Wisdom for a Changing Business World*. New York: Warner Books, 1991.

Leonard, Linda Schierse. *On the Way to the Wedding: Transforming the Love Relationship*. Boston: Shambala Books, 1986.

Maclean, Norman. *A River Runs Through It*. Chicago: The University Press, 1976.

Maser, Chris. *The Redesigned Forest*. Toronto: Stoddard, 1990.

---

*For children, as well as adults.

McLerran, Alice, and Eric Castle. *The Mountain That Loved a Bird*. Saxonville, MD: Picture Book Studio, 1985.*

Miller, Alice. *The Untouched Key, Tracing Childhood Trauma in Creativity and Destructiveness*. Toronto: Doubleday, 1990.

Miller, D. *The Icarus Paradox: How Excellent Companies Bring About Their Own Downfall*. London: Harper Collins, 1990.

Mitchell, Stephen. *Genesis: A New Translation of the Classical Biblical Stories*. New York: Harper Collins, 1996.

Morgan, Marlo. *Mutant Message Down Under*. San Francisco: Harper Collins, 1995.

Moyers, Bill. *Genesis, A Living Conversation*. New York: Doubleday, 1996.

Munsch, Robert, and Michael Martchenko. *The Paperbag Princess*. Toronto: Annick Press, 1980.*

New Oxford Annotated Bible. New York: Oxford University Press, 1991.

O'Collins, Gerald. *The Second Journey, Spiritual Awareness and the Mid-Life Crisis*. New York: Paulist Press, 1978.

Peters, Tom. *Thriving on Chaos*. New York: Alfred A Knopf, 1987.

Pitzele, Peter. *Our Fathers' Wells, A Personal Encounter With the Myths of Genesis*. San Francisco: Harper, 1995.

Sacks, Oliver. *An Anthropologist on Mars*. Toronto: Random House, 1996.

Schell, Jonathan. *The Fate of the Earth*. New York: Avon Books, 1982.

Sheehy, Gail. *New Passages: Mapping Your Life Across Time*. New York: Random House, 1995.

Smye, Mardi. *Is It Too Late To Run Away and Join the Circus?* Toronto: Key Porter Books, 1998.

Sullivan, Francis Patrick. *Tragic Psalms*. Washington, DC: The Pastoral Press, 1987.

Walker, Kelly. *Loss of Soul: Burnout*. Oakville: KW Productions, 1997.

Westermann, C. *Genesis 1-11*. Minneapolis: Augsburg Publishing House, 1984.

Wheatley, M.J. *Leadership and the New Science: Learning about Organizations from an Orderly Universe*. San Francisco: Berrett-Koekler, 1992.

Wycoff, Joyce. *Mindmapping, Your Personal Guide to Exploring Creativity and Problem Solving*. New York: Berkley Books, 1991.

Yalom, Irvin D. *When Nietzche Wept*. New York: Harper Perennial, 1992.

Yehl Marta, Suzie. *The Single Symphony: A Single Parent Grief Guide*. Rolling Meadows, IL: Rainbows, 1996. 1-800-266-3206, or www.rainbows.org.

Young, Jeffrey E., and Janet S. Klosko. *Reinventing Your Life, How to Break Free from Negative Life Patterns and Feel Good Again*. New York: Plume Books, 1994.

APPENDIX
Food for your Journey

Eternal Spirit,
Earth-Maker, Pain Bearer, Life-Giver,
Source of all that is and shall be,
Father and Mother of us all,
Loving God in whom is heaven:
The hallowing of your name echo through the universe!

The way of your justice be followed by the peoples of the world!
Your heavenly will be done by all created beings!
Your commonwealth of peace and freedom
sustain our hope and come on earth.

With the bread we need for today, feed us.
In the hurts we absorb from one another, forgive us.
In times of temptation and test, strengthen us.

From trials too great to endure, spare us.
From the grip of all that is evil, free us.
For you reign in the glory of the power that is love
now and forever. Amen.

—From the New Zealand Prayer Book of the Anglican Church.

• • •

Psalm 137

The bitter songs we sang as captives
crouched by the river in Babylon, remember!
How we hid our harps in the thick trees not to play our lyrics of
joy for them.

They goaded us, "Sing something happy, songs about your
God!"

*It was torment! What lyrics of God would they not profane if we
sang them!*

*Jerusalem, if I ever do, may the hand that plays be paralysed,
and may I choke
If ever, if you, Jerusalem, do not look proud worn on my head
like a wreath on a holy day! God! Our blood kin too wanted
Jerusalem ruined:
"Strip her down to the last rag of stone!"*

*Remember! It would be a fierce joy for me, Babylon, you greedy
beast,
To see you sacked ounce for ounce as you once sacked us, a fierce
joy for me if someone took your young as you did ours and
brained them on the rocks!*

—From Tragic Psalms

•   •   •

De Profundis

*From the pits I cry to you.
Where? Where have you been?
From down deep in the deepest part of my sadness
comes the howl
that creeps through the crevices
of pain
and breaks the coal
cold crepiscules
that keep my babe out of arms
from light.*

*Where is the face that knows me
that cherishes my entrails and my breath?
Where is the hand that fashioned me
from vapour and a seed
into time and dance...*

Where is the womb that bore me
into a frame whose picture
I still do not know...

Where is the breath
that spiralled me into
time
and
time
again?

For now I am awakening
to horizons that end
somehow
in space
in time
in imagination
and catapult me
with all that I have claimed
into a whatever.
Hear my call!

—*Kelly Walker*

• • •

Nomad

When I look inside of me, I wonder how I feel.
When I look beyond the rim, I wonder why it's raining.
When I look to open skies, I wonder who is there.
When I look through broken clouds, I wonder who is listening.

Are you just a word that someone spoke to us one broken night?
Or are you just a figment of imaginary grasping in the dark?
A friend? An answer to a prayer?
A new day? A dawning in my life?

Hands of our are hand that grab the gun before the flute.

Arms that blow up little ones, that suit the broken harmony,
The cry into the night...
Are we all still living here, or dying deaths, no energy to fight
for life?

Come and pitch your tent with us, O Nomad of the Days.
Come and fill our broken hearts, O Bearer of new Mays.
Springtime for all Humankind, be with us now, we pray.

No longer far...
No name obscured...
Be radiant as the day!

—*Kelly Walker, from Nomad*

• • •

The change in a painter's life due to oncoming blindness

When the author of this book, Kelly Walker, asked me to write about the change in my life caused by approaching blindness and its consequent effect on my work as an artist, I felt it would be good for me to examine this in writing. It was in one sense a calamity, but I can also look back at the positive things that happened to my working process in the twelve years or so that elapsed between the onset of muscular degeneration until I was registered, in 1997, at the age of 70, as a blind person.

I stopped painting at the end of 1996 because I could no longer judge the quality of anything I produced, and therefore could not "publish" any new work.

I had a conventional training as an art student, but right from the very beginning of my awareness as an artist I was excited by what is loosely termed "modernism." At a very early stage of my career I wanted to learn about cubism, surrealism, and more. In fact I left the Byam Shaw School in London, because they would not consider even the importance of a painter like Cezanne, and consequently they felt that cubism was a blind alley in the development of modern painting.

Eventually, I selected the Central School of Art and Design in London where most of the British *avant-garde* were teaching. Although the School emphasized the necessity of drawing and painting from the figure and from still life, as a student I was open to all the current ideas and attitudes that prevailed among the diverse interests of the professional artists who were teaching there.

I graduated and practiced professionally as an abstract painter for some twenty years, while also teaching at various art schools and university departments. Then around 1976 I turned to look at nature and began to express myself in my work through looking at the natural world.

Statistically, only 7% of registered blind people are completely without any kind of vision at all. To be told, at the age of 58, when my whole life depended on a visual stimulus and to a great extent visual information, that I was suffering from an incurable eye disease, was a blow that felt a tragedy of the first kind.

In the early and middle stages of my partial blindness, I was to some degree assisted by optical aids, from spectacles to magnifiers. Gradually, the stimulus I had experienced all through my life closed down and, after an initial period, which was rather depressing and sad, I realized that something was beginning to happen in my work as a painter that had a positive side.

People viewing my work commented on the quality of colour and how strong it was. With the loss of middle and distant focus, I had to rely on photographic reference for my information in the paintings. Very soon after the knowledge of approaching blindness, through constant examination of the light and movement of a river, which was twenty feet from my studio door in Shepperton, Surrey, I found that I was becoming more and more interested in the broken rhythms of distorted reflections and I attempted to do something about this when painting.

Eventually, in order to see what I was doing I had to enlarge the format of my paintings. Inevitably, because my sight was deteriorating and I needed the largeness of marks to comprehend what was happening on the canvas, I had to reinvent the means of application of the paint to become aware of and to perceive what I was doing. This led me to a completely different method of isolating an experience, and consequently some of the best work I have ever created happened in the last five or six years.

Personally, my life is deeply affected by blunted vision. This is where I have experienced a loss of independence and self-confidence to some degree in the tackling of everyday jobs and events. Travelling has become difficult unless accompanied, and traffic is much more of a hazard than before when walking.

Recognizing people in social gatherings and in the street has become progressively difficult. Tradesmen have to be employed to do many of the simple repair operations around the house that I previously would have done. A simple operation for a male of urinating into a conventional toilet became a hazard and I need to disrobe to avoid any problems occurring.

There are innumerable other consequences of approaching blindness such as, at an early stage, being unable to drive a car anymore, and, at a later stage, being unable to read the written word, or see to write. So many of the activities that I once associated with very simple tasks and took for granted are no longer possible.

Then there is the problem of one's relationship with one's family and friends. One automatically comes to rely on the assistance of one's nearest and dearest and if the relationship is less than loving, one would be in deep trouble. Fortunately, I do not have this problem because my wife is totally supportive. She is helpful to a degree of great sacrifice, in order to make life bearable and indeed creative. There is never anything that is too much trouble for her.

As one experiences the disappearance of the ability to execute the simplest of tasks, for example writing and using simple tools, this creates problems of frustration and lack of confidence. One feels alone and almost imprisoned by an ability to live as one did before the event of blunted vision. This obstacle is very difficult to overcome, and to maintain an optimistic view of one's life at this point seems almost impossible.

In order to survive one has to rebuild and, I feel, one has to accept the condition as almost normal. In a way one must try to live not through what one had and would have liked to do before the onset of blindness, but totally within the condition that one finds oneself in now. It is important not to envy the capability of sighted people. One becomes a different animal. I often think of myself in relation to animals with poor sight like bats and moles. You have to live within the means with which you are presented.

When my sight was deteriorating I applied this attitude to my process of working as well. One condition helped the other. The crossover of these conditions is difficult to describe, but with the help of a close partner, one can still enjoy living almost as much as possibly one did before.

—*John Plumb, December, 1997*

Kelly Walker's CD, *River Ash*, sixteen of his own piano improvisations, is dedicated to John Plumb. The artwork entitled, "Autumn Reflections in the River Ash," was chosen as a cover for this CD.